Boosting Population-Health Literacy Through Intervention

Dr. Kalawati Jaiswal
Reader & Head,
Department of Psychology,
Marwari College,
Ranchi University, Ranchi, India

ACKNOWLEDGEMENTS

From the core of my heart, I acknowledge the cooperation and help of my Supervisor, **Dr. Shahid Hassan**, Former Head and Associate Professor, Post-graduate Department of Psychology, Ranchi University, Ranchi. In spite of his busy schedule in social and academic activities, he was kind enough to spare his precious time for the review of this book. He guided me at every stage of my research work. My words can't express the feelings that I have for him.

I am thankful to **Mrs. Rekha Tripathy**, Head of the Post-graduate Department of Psychology, Ranchi University, Ranchi and **Dr. (Mrs.) Bharati Roy**, Former Head of the Post-graduate Department of Psychology, Ranchi University, Ranchi who were kind enough to help me at every stage of my research. I can't forget their inspiring and encouraging words.

I express my sincere regards and respect to my Principal, **Dr. Javed Ahmed**, for the promotion towards my research work for this book and also inspiring me from time to time towards the completion of the book.

I am extremely thankful to **Dr. Indira Rai,** Ex-Professor-in-Charge and Head, Department of Psychology, Marwari College,

Ranchi, for her invaluable cooperation, moral support and guidance towards the completion of this book. She always stood by my side and inspired me through the course of this research.

Sincere help rendered to me by **Dr. Meera Jayaswal**, PG Department of Psychology, in different capacities can hardly go unnoticed by me. I thank her again.

I am thankful to **Late. Dr. M. K. Hassan**, Ex-University Professor of Psychology, Head & Dean of Social-Sciences, for his queries about the research and his advices with regard to the concerned problems.

I am equally thankful to **Late. Dr. Enayatullah**, Ex-University Professor of Psychology, Head & Dean of Social-Sciences, Vinoba Bhave University, for his incessant guidance and support throughout the research and publication of this book.

I express my sincere thanks to **Dr. S. K. Sinha,** Ex-University Professor of Psychology, Head & Dean of Social-Sciences, for his cooperation and suggestions in matter of my research work. However much I praise him, it's not enough.

I have full regards for **Dr. Abdul Khalique,** PG Department of Psychology, for sparing his valuable time in giving me proper advice and suitable suggestions from time to time during the course of my research work. I am equally thankful to **Dr. Renu** iii

Dewan, **Dr. Shashikala Singh** and **Dr. Anita Arora**, PG Department of Psychology, for their support and cooperation during my research work.

I shall be failing in my duty if I don't remember at this moment my closest friend **Dr. Neelam Verma**, Department of Psychology, R.K Mahila College, Giridih, for her purified blessings and moral support at different steps of my research work. Expression of my thanks and gratitude towards her, I feel, will carry less weight than her concern about my work.

I am indebted to my husband **Dr. Shree Kant Prasad**, Assistant Professor in Commerce, S.S Memorial College, Ranchi, for helping me in writing my book. Writing this thesis would have been a distant dream for me without his cooperation in each and every step, be it the selection of the problems, data collection or other related works. I am short of words to express my gratitude towards him. My son, **Vaibhav**, MBA from IIM Calcutta and an Engineer from MIT Manipal, laughed it off when I expressed my feelings about his help in completing this book. Similarly my daughter, **Parul**, made sincere efforts and helped me towards the collation of data. I am once again thankful to both my children.

The other family members, particularly **Sri Basant Kumar Jaiswal, Mrs. Indu Jaiswal** & **Dr. Usha Suwalka**, Head, iv

Department of Anaesthesia, Rajendra Institute of Medical Sciences, Ranchi, deserve my sincere gratitude for their moral encouragement towards my efforts with regard to this book.

I am also obliged to **Dr. Shriti Choudhary**, Assistant Professor, Department of Psychology, R. L. S. Y. College, Ranchi, for using her Questionnaire and Population-Health Literacy Material in my research.

I am especially thankful to **Sri Ramjee Prasad** for typing this voluminous book, beautifully, in a record time.

My sincere thanks go to my all other colleagues and staffs who have helped me in any way during the process of publication of this book.

And last but not least, my heartfelt gratitude to **ALL the participants** of my study and their family members who cooperated during the process.

DR. KALAWATI JAISWAL

Reader & Head,
Department of Psychology,
Marwari College,
Ranchi University,
Ranchi, India

Contents

LIST OF TABLES

viii

LIST OF FIGURES

CHAPTER 1

1   INTRODUCTION

1.1   THE PROBLEM

The present book envisages analysing the Population-Health Literacy (PHL) of educated Hindu women of Ranchi in Socio-Psychological perspective. PHL is essential for the people of India in general and for the females in particular. It is expected in a developed, civilized and healthy society that the people are aware of their health related issues. Women, on priority basis, should have the knowledge of how to conceive, what care should be taken during pregnancy, delivery and post-delivery maintenance. Women should know the common children-related diseases, their preventions, immunization, and should also have knowledge about child care. Increased population has produced several population related problems in our country. One should be aware of the suitable age for marriage, conceiving a child, gap between two children and the size of the family, as well as the methods of avoiding unnecessary pregnancy and the abortive measures if needed. The knowledge related to all these matters may be labelled as 'Population-Health Literacy'. With the application of psychology in the area of health, the concept of PHL has attracted the attention of social scientists and psychologists. A new branch of psychology emerged out of it and is called 'Health Psychology'.

The present problem is an effort to know the status of educated women in Population-Health Literacy, whether the general education serves in the increase of Population-Health Literacy or not. Another aspect of the problem is whether increasing age has any relation with Population-Health Literacy or not. Thus, education and age have been used as sociological factors of Population-Health Literacy.

Yet another aspect of Population-Health Literacy has also been examined, that is, whether intervention influences the level of Population-Health Literacy or not. For intervention, specially constructed Population-Health Education materials have been used as a psychological variable. An experimental design has been used to examine the effect of intervention on Population-Health Literacy. Both single-group and double-group designs have been used. In the single-group design, the level of Population-Health Literacy has been measured both before and after the intervention and both the responses have been compared. To locate and avoid the effect of first response on the second response, a two-group design has also been used to examine where one group works as the Control Group and the other group works as an Experimental Group. Both the groups are well-matched before intervention. The intervention programme has been exposed to Experimental Group only. The responses of Control Group have been tested before and after (no intervention given to this group) intervention to Experimental Group only. The Experimental Group has been tested both before and after intervention. The comparison of the first and the second responses of Control Group have shown the impact of first response on the second, while the comparison of the first and the second responses of the Experimental Group have given an idea of the real effect of intervention. So, a well-planned experimental design has been used in determining the effect of intervention on Population-Health Literacy of educated women.

Thus, the present problem is based on the determination of the effects of these socio-psychological variables on Population-Health Literacy.

1.2 POPULATION EXPLOSION: A THREAT TO INDIA

Rising population, especially post-independence, emerged as the most urgent and concerning problem in India. Singh (1984) pointed out 3 Ps as threat to our nation: Population, Poverty and

Prejudice. He analysed their dehumanising consequences and also marked all the three Ps as inter-related to each other.

Prior to 300 BC, there is no estimation about population of India. Between 300 BC and 1600 AD, the population of India seems to be stationary – neither much increase nor much decrease was noticed. A record shows India's population around 255 million in 1871 which declined to 251 million in 1921, as there were epidemics like influenza and the great famine during 1911-1920. The beginning of accelerated growth is marked since 1951 and the next six decades so far. After independence in 1947, the advances in medical technology resulted in a decrease in death rate and increase in longevity. 1961 decade saw an increase of 21.64 percent while the 1971, 1981 and 1991 decades marked 24.8, 24.66 and 23.87 percent rises respectively. Table 1.1 in the next page shows the trend.

Table - 1.1

Population trend in India (1901-2011) Birth rate, Death rate and Growth rate

Year	Population In Million	Crude Birth Rate	Crude Death Rate	Percentage Decadal Variation	Average Annual Exponential Growth Rate
1901	238.4	--	--	--	--
1911	252.1	49.2	42.6	5.75	0.56
1921	251.3	48.1	47.2	-0.31	-0.03
1931	278.9	46.4	36.3	11.00	1.04
1941	318.7	45.2	31.2	14.22	1.33
1951	361.1	39.9	27.4	13.31	1.25
1961	439.2	41.7	22.8	21.64	1.96
1971	548.2	41.2	19.0	24.80	2.20
1981	683.3	37.2	15.0	24.66	2.22
1991	846.4	29.5	9.8	23.87	2.16
2001	1028.7	26.0	8.5	21.54	1.97
2011	1210.2	20.9	7.5	17.64	1.64

SOURCE:

Registrar General of India, Census Figures, Registrar General, India, India 2011
CIA World Fact-book, July, 2011

The alarm signals given by 1971 and 1981 census remained unheeded because of the highly irresponsible behaviour of the political leadership (Banerji, 1992: 883). The 1991 census recorded a decadal increase of 160.7 million in the Indian population, almost equal to the combined population of France, UK and Italy

(Srinivasan, 1991: 3). A Draft National Population Policy, 1994 estimated population over 1,000 million by 2000 (Srinivisan, K. 1995: 296-97). According to another estimate, the population would increase to approximately 2.5 billion around 2040 (Conly and Camp, 1992). Such a spiral growth has been labelled as 'Exponential Growth' and illustrated by the example of the Pond Weed:

> *A classic example used to illustrate this is the pond weed that doubles each day the amount of pond surface covered and is projected to cover the entire pond in 30 days. The question is, how much of the pond will be covered in twenty nine days? The answer, of course, is that just half of the pond will be covered in twenty nine days. The weed will then double once more and cover the entire pond the next day.*

Ehrlich and Ehrlich (1990:15)

1.2.1 Population Explosion: Adverse Consequences

Rapid growth of population has a negative effect on the pace of human development. Trakroo, P.L (1999) stated:

> *Population and development of any society are interrelated. A galloping growth rate in population threatens the precarious balance between natural resource and the*

people. It threatens availability of basic necessities like health-care, drinking water, food, shelter, education, sanitation. During the last five decades, a paradigm shift from growth to development has brought into focus the need for conversion of 'human resource' to 'human capital' for nation building.

Rapid growth of population has its effect on the basic needs of the people, creating many problems, some of which are listed below.

Food problem

Though India has a better status than what it had been in the 1960s, additional annual increase in population means that India requires additional production of 12 crores 54 lakh 530 tonnes of food grains. Borlaug (1990), winner of Nobel Prize for peace for his invention of high yielding wheat-seed which helped Green Revolution in India, has warned that the present food sufficiency has given only a temporary respite and the population explosion may offset the gain.

Water scarcity

Due to over population, water consumption has increased. The situation has reached a level of crisis in big cities, as documented by *The Hindu Survey of the Environment* (1994). In

1993, Delhi, Bombay and Ahmadabad had gaps of water supply of 695, 912 and 212 mld respectively (NIUA, 1994).

Shelter problem

The rapid growth of population has increased the problem of housing. The growth of population has increased the urban population creating thickly populated slums in and around mega cities. If the population continues in such a way, after 900 years only one square yard of land will be available for a person (Ehrlich, 1968).

Population and Urbanisation

The urban population is growing steadily. According to an estimate, 55% of the total population of Bombay lives in 2641 slums; one of these slums is *Dharavi* - the largest slum in Asia. The other big cities of India also have a large percentage of slum population: Kolkata and Chennai (35), Delhi (32.8) and Ahmadabad (30). This population thickness is creating physical and psychological illnesses too. About 30% of the population of Delhi is prone to respiratory problems (Sharma, 1993).

Population and Environment

About 1.33 million hectares of forests are destroyed each year to meet the needs of food, shelter and fuel of the additional population (Varshney, 1991: 151).

Rapid growth of urbanisation and industrialization are causing air and water pollution. The disposal of human and industrial wastes is polluting the river water. The environmental problems such as water pollution and water scarcity, air pollution, solid and hazardous wastes, soil degradation, deforestation, loss of biodiversity and atmospheric changes have bearing on health, which in turn, adversely affects productivity (UN 1994: 6).

Population and Employment

The number of unemployed persons has also increased due to population increase. In 1992, there were 17 million unemployed people and another 6 million people were severely under-employed.

Population and Literacy/Education

With increased population, the need for education has also increased. A large section of society, which exists below the poverty line or around this, cannot afford the educational expenses fixed by the private schools. The centre for Policy Research, New Delhi estimated the overall educational budget between Rs. 38,000 crores to Rs. 49,000 crores (Malgavkar, 1991).

1.2.2   Population Planning In India

Time-to-time, there are reports of the schemes that India has planned for controlling the population. Indian history reveals that mythological views favoured the bigger size of family. During ancient times, the most preferred blessing in India used to be *"May you be the mother of hundred sons"*. But there are also a few instances which favoured a smaller family. According to *Rigveda*, a man with many children succumbs to miseries (Das, B. 1975).

The real population may be traced back to the 1891 census when the famous economist and demographer, T. R. Malthus commented that India's poverty was a consequence of over-population. R. D. Karve started Birth Control Movement at Girgaun in Bombay in 1921. Indian Birth Control Society was formed in 1922 by Gopaljee Ahluwalia in Delhi and N. S. Phadke started the Birth-Control League in Bombay in 1923. Neo-Malthusian League was formed in Chennai. First Birth Control clinic was established by the Government of Mysore in 1930.

Post-Independence India took many steps for controlling population in India. National Planning Committee constituted a sub-committee for this purpose. In 1949, Family Planning Association of India was established by Dhanwanti Rama Rao. In 1960, family planning was related with family welfare. This worked for the quality of life (Banerji, 1980). Dr. Karan Singh, the then Minister for Health and Family Planning, declared the National Population Policy (1976). In 1976, by the 42nd amendment to the Constitution of

India, family planning was included in the concurrent list. Forced sterilization was adopted during national emergency by Sanjay Gandhi, the son of the Late Prime Minister, Mrs. Indira Gandhi (Bose, 1988). Because of the considerable overlap of population and health issues, it seems appropriate to discuss the National Health Policy of Govt. of India.

> *Irrespective of the changes, no matter how fundamental, that may be brought about in the overall approach to health-care and the restructuring of the health services, not much headway is likely to be achieved in improving the health status of the people unless success is achieved in securing the small family norm, through voluntary efforts and moving towards the goal of population stabilisation in view of the vital importance of securing the balanced growth of the population. It is necessary to enunciate separately a National Population Policy.*

> GOI (1982: 5)

The Swaminathan Committee was constituted for the formulation of a National Population Policy. The report of the Committee was submitted in 1994 and the said policy was approved by the Union Cabinet in 2000. Population issues remain there in every Five-Year plan from the first Five-Year Plan (1951-1956) till the Eleventh Five-Year Plan (2007-2012).

All the family planning/policies could not work properly during the first four decades after independence. Though these had positive effects afterwards, the gain is slow.

1.2.3   Barriers to Population Planning

Despite all attempts, ways, planning and policies, India could not successfully control the rapid growth of population in the first few decades after independence for which she is still suffering. The following barriers worked as great hurdles in the way of controlling population.

Illiteracy, particularly Female Illiteracy

Female Literacy has a significant correlation with the Infant Mortality Rate (IMR) and the Total Fertility Rate (TFR). Higher the Female Literacy Rate, lower is the Fertility Rate and the Infant Mortality Rate. This has been proved in Kerala. Bihar, Madhya Pradesh, Rajasthan and Uttar Pradesh have the lowest female literacy rates and these states contribute 42% of the total population of India and they were labelled as BIMARU (sick states).

Poverty

The poor do not share the perception of the elite that population growth is an important issue. The poor constitute 35% of the Indian population (Panandiker and Umashankar, 1994). Large family size is perceived by them as being advantageous. They feel their children should help in domestic works, grazing cattle, collecting wood for fuel and sale. Both male and female children are perceived equally for doing these works as they do not bother for their proper education.

Son Preference

Male child is the preferred child in Indian society, irrespective of religion, region and SES. Some families want a son even after having two or three daughters. The son is considered the carrier of family name and heir of the ancestral property. If gender preferences could be eliminated entirely, the fertility level in India would decline by about 8 percent.

The Electoral Politics

The caste and religion based politics in India imposes an idea in the minds of the people that if they will be lesser in number, they might be excluded from the political participation - because in democracy, the number matters.

Corruption and Inefficiency

With the recent spate of corruption allegations against the ruling party, corruption in the form of huge scams and also petty briberies has been at its peak. The population planning and policies are worked out in papers only. Most of the data shown by the block and district offices are based on false reporting to show achievements.

Corruption has become the most talked about issue in 2011. The virus of corruption has infected almost every sphere of the Indian society.

1.2.4   How to Stabilise Population?

Development has been considered to be a vital instrument for population stabilisation. Singh (1975) has argued that education and economic development will result in low fertility.

Population Control: A combination of several factors

Several factors have been working as barriers to family planning. A combination of all the factors can bring stability in population.

Family Planning Services and Quality of Care

Townsend (1994) and Carlson (1994) have underlined the importance of women empowerment, female literacy, and reduction in IMR, meeting unmet demands and improving quality of services in fertility reduction. Care quality should be developed.

Population Control: Reproductive and Child Health (RCH)

The International Conference on Population and Development (ICPD), 1994 held at Cairo compelled the social scientists, doctors, workers in the field of family planning for application of a global programme including universally accepted human rights standards to all the aspects of population control programme. The programme should be need-based, client-centred, demand-driven, and consideration-oriented for child-care, women-care, sexual-needs of males and females, ways of birth control and different aspects of children.

Reproductive and Child Health Care (RCH) Programme in India

India adopted Family Welfare Programmes in a reproductive and child health perspective (World Bank, 1995). Prior to this programme the women came in the focus of attention of the Government only after her pregnancy and disappeared after menopause. In this new approach of Reproductive and Health Care (RCH) a woman is considered as a full human being. The programme covers the well-being of every stage of her life - from birth to death.

The RCH programme aims to provide need-based, client-centred, demand-driven, high quality mother and child health services instead of target oriented and method specific approach of family planning and Family Welfare Programme.

Thus, reproductive health is a crucial part of general health, particularly of women. It also incorporates child health which is an integral part of women's health.

Reproductive and child health programme in India aims to improve quality and coverage of health care to women, children and adolescents, so that their felt needs for health care can be fully met. Comprehensive reproductive and child health care will promote:

- Effective maternal and child health care to ensure safe motherhood and child survival
- Increased access to contraceptive care to prevent unwanted pregnancies
- Larger abortion facilities for safe management of unwanted pregnancies
- Effective nutritional services to vulnerable groups
- Reproductive health services for adolescents

- Prevention and treatment of gynaecological problems including infertility, menstruation disorder and prolapsed uterus

- Screening and treatment of cancers, especially that of uterine, cervix and breast (Government of India, Ninth Five Year Plan 1997-2002)

The Government of India had decided the expected levels of achievements by the year 2002 through this programme. The goals are given in the table below (Table 1.2):

Table - 1.2

Reproductive and Child Care (RCH) Programme:

Expected Level of Achievements by 2002

Sl. No.	Major States/UT (Population more than 1 crore)	IMR	CBR	NMR	TFR	CPR
1	Andhra Pradesh	60-53	20-18	35	2.3-2.1	55-70
2	Assam	60-55	25-22	35	2.7-2.5	30-40
3	Bihar	50-44	27-25	35	4.0-3.0	30-45
4	Gujarat	40-35	22-20	35	2.5-2.2	65-75

5	Haryana	50-45	27-23	35	3.0-2.5	60-70
6	Karnataka	60-50	21-20	35	2.4-2.1	60-70
7	Kerala	10-09	16-15	09	1.7-1.6	60-70
8	Madhya Pradesh	80-70	29-25	50	3.5-2.8	60-70
9	Maharashtra	41-36	20-17	35	2.5-2.2	65-65
10	Orissa	90-70	25-21	50	2.7-2.4	60-70
11	Punjab	44-40	21-18	20	2.5-2.2	45-55
12	Rajasthan	56-50	28-24	40	3.5-3.0	82-85
13	Tamil Nadu	39-35	18-16	20	1.9-1.7	40-50
14	Uttar Pradesh	75-60	30-26	40	3.8-3.4	60-70
15	West Bengal	51-46	24-20	30	2.6-2.4	50-55
	All India	56-50	24-23	35	2.9-2.6	51-60

SOURCE:
Government of India (1997) *Ninth Five Year Plan (1997-2002) Volume II, Thematic Issues and Sectoral Programmes.* Planning Commission, New Delhi

IMR = Infant Mortality Rate   CBR = Crude Birth Rate   NMR = Neonatal Mortality Rate   TFR = Total Fertility Rate   CPR = Couple Protection Rate

This paradigm shift from Family Welfare to Reproductive and Child Health approach puts a challenge to the Indian programme designers and managers. The success of the programme depends upon its honest and efficient implementation at all levels – from top policy makers to grass-root beneficiaries.

1.3 POPULATION EDUCATION: THE CONCEPT

Population education has been misconceived with family planning programme or sex education or family life education. Social scientists have felt difficulties in conceptualisation of the term, National Council for Educational Research and Training (NCERT), in its draft syllabus on Population education, has explained population education as:

> *...an educational innovation aimed at making the target groups aware about the inter-relationship between population and development. It endeavours to bring the idea home that the decisions taken by every person in respect of population phenomena at individual, community, societal and national levels affect the cause of development and the status of the individual and national quality of life. It is basically an education in human resource development. The ultimate objective of this education is to bring about an attitudinal change in the people towards such socio-cultural norms, traditional beliefs and values that promote pro-natality among them and prevent an*

articulate appreciation of development perspective. It is hoped that by doing so, population education will enable its target groups to take rational decisions regarding population issues.

Quoted by Parakh and Pandey (1991: 33-34)

Population education is an educational programme. Its need was first advocated by Alva Myrdal in 1941 in USA, referred as family education by her. Columbia University prepared the education materials for it. Later the need of Population Education was felt and accepted by WHO, UNFPA, UNICEF, UNDP and the World Bank.

The importance was later accepted by the Government of India in its various documents such as National Population Policy (1976), Family Welfare Programme (1977) and Draft National Population Policy (1994).

The concept of population overlaps with that of health. Both are separate concepts but both can be combined. Population education is a wider concept and embraces all aspects of population which affect the quality of life, most importantly health. Thus the component of population education inevitably contains substantial health education.

If one analyses, one will find the importance of Population-Health Education in Human Development in a country like India. Poverty and illiteracy also seem to be associated with it. Singh, A. K. et al. (1987), after analysing the whole affairs existing in our country, rightly mentioned:

> *Recent developments in medical sciences have provided information and technologies which are so simple that an illiterate can understand them, so inexpensive that a poor person can afford them, so complete that every individual can self-administer them without the expert guidance of doctors and so effective that a significant reduction in malnutrition and illness and death and disability can be achieved. These health information and technologies are related to diarrhoeal diseases and respiratory infections, immunisation and monitoring the growth of the child, diet and nutrition, cleanliness of food and water, personal hygiene and environmental sanitation, birth control and birth spacing, breast feeding and supplementary food for children at the weaning age.*

> Singh, A. K. et al. (1987a: 10)

Accepting the facts above makes one feel the need for obtaining the Population-Health Education. In other words, it suggests an idea of Population-Health Literacy, especially in India.

Population-Health Literacy (PHL)

The concept of Population-Health Literacy (PHL) has been suggested for Population-Health Education. The PHL may be defined as the:

> *Scientifically correct information, attitudes and behaviour in relation to population and health issues conducive to rational and effective living and a necessary pre-requisite for human and social development. PHL is the fundamental core-content of Population-Health Education and its pre-requisite as literacy, the knowledge of three Rs is for general education.*

> Singh, A. K. et al. (1988: 11)

Thus, the PHL is the basic rudiment or the ABC of Population-Health Education.

Contents used in the Population-Health Literacy

The contents for the measurement of PHL have been used as suggested by Singh et al. (1988). There are 10 dimensions, each dimension is based on five themes and each dimension is measured by 10 most-similar type items. The following dimensions/themes have been used:

1. Adverse Consequences of Population Explosion

   - Magnitude of population growth in India

   - Birth-rate and death-rate

   - Factors affecting quality of life

   - Effect of population explosion on health, education, employment and environment

   - Measures for population control: types of contraceptives

2. Timing Birth

   - Appropriate duration between births of two children

   - Appropriate child-bearing age

   - Number of children after which pregnancy is dangerous for mother

   - Effect of subsequent pregnancy on the health of mother and child

   - Time required for recovery after pregnancy and child birth

   - Pregnancy in young age: disadvantages and measures to check it

3. Safe Motherhood

   - Child birth: attended by trained or traditional health-worker

- Food and rest for mother during pregnancy

- Weight-gain during pregnancy

- Signs of danger during pregnancy

- Regular check-ups during pregnancy

- Minimum weight of the mother before pregnancy and minimum weight gain during pregnancy

- Common physical complications during pregnancy

4. Breast Feeding

- Qualities of breast-milk

- When to start breast-feeding and till when should it be continued

- How to ensure adequate breast milk

- Physical position of the mother and child at the time of breast-feeding

- Psychological aspects of breast-feeding

- Breast-feeding during illness of the child and mother

- Working mother and breast-feeding, bottle feeding versus breast-feeding, alternatives of breast-feeding

5. Immunisation

- Advantages of immunisation

- Immunisation schedule

- Diseases due to lack of immunisation

- Booster dose of the main medicine

- Physical reactions after immunisation and their cure

- Necessity of tetanus vaccines for the mother and child

6. Supplementary Food

   - Need of supplementary food for the baby

   - Appropriate age for providing supplementary food to the baby

   - Contents and methods for preparing supplementary food

   - Frequency of giving supplementary food to the baby

7. Child Growth

   - Correct method of monitoring child's weight

   - Regular assessment of growth

   - Duration of weight monitoring

   - Causes of no-weight gain and measures to be taken to overcome it

   - Food for the child after illness

   - Psychological development of the child

   - Role of play in child's life

8. Hygiene

    - Advantages of cleaning hands, cleaning of child's face

    - Defecation habits of children and adults

    - Cleanliness of food and water

    - Cleanliness of home and village

9. Diarrhoea

    - Measures taken after loss of water from the body

    - Oral Rehydration Therapy: preparation and application

    - Food and water during diarrhoea

    - Signs of dehydration

10. Coughs and Colds

    - Conversion of coughs and colds into pneumonia

    - Children more susceptible to pneumonia

    - Signs of pneumonia and precautionary measures

    - Food and liquid intake during coughs and colds

    - Method of keeping a child comfortable during coughs and colds

CHAPTER 2

2 REVIEW OF LITERATURE

The ignorance about Population-Health Education is an obstacle in the process of population control and other health related issues. Most of the studies have tried to correlate the factors associated with inappropriate population control in spite of all public propaganda and attempts. It has been considered that there is a need to re-educate the people with appropriate teaching materials.

Several studies in India have reported that people do not put a control on their fertility due to ignorance and misconceptions on health and population related issues (Arora and Choudhary, 1993; Basu, 1984; Rajyalaxmi, 1991; Singh and Jayaswal, 1989; Singh and Jayaswal, 1995). One of the interesting aspects of these findings is the fact that ignorance and misconceptions are not only prevalent among the poor and illiterate but they are widespread among literates too, such as college students (Choudhary and Singh, 1994).

The ignorance and misconceptions can be eliminated through appropriate intervention or education. Educating people can bring a change in their attitudes, approaches leading to positive behaviour to population education and control, and healthy life.

Most of the studies on Population-Health Education have been done to determine the role of intervention programmes in increasing the level of Population-Health Literacy. The studies include major themes of mother and child care, diet and nutrition, personal hygiene and environmental sanitation, physical and mental health as well as very specific topics like human organ-donation (Ganikos, M. L. et al. 1994), occupation related diseases such as those caused by exposure to lead (Porru, S. et al. 1993), local specific diseases, as for example Schistosomiasis (Schall, V. T. et al. 1993) and Helminthic (Das Santos, M. G. et al. 1993) in Brazil and control of *Redes aegypti* in Mexico (Lloyd, L. S. et al. 1994). PHEI studies have been done on specific important diseases with very large prevalence such as arthritis (Lorig, K. R. et al. 1993) tuberculosis (Meincke-Giebrecht et al. 1993; Salleras, 1993), cervical cancer (Dhamija, S. et al. 1993) and testicular cancer (Rosella, 1994), parasitic diseases (Akogun, O. B. 1992) and intestinal infection (Odonsi, J. K. and Ogan, V. N. 1993). The PHEI studies have been done on comprehensive programmes such as Comprehensive School Health Education and Growing Health Programme in USA (Brindis 1993, Waller and Goldman 1993) and school Health Education in the European Community (Williams, T. and Jones, H. 1993). On the other hand, PHEI has been done on a particular health habit such as tooth-brushing behaviour (Paunio, P. et al. 1994), defecation habits (Murthy, G. V. et al. 1990), and hand washing (Wilson, J. M. et al. 1994). PHEI studies have also been taken on a broad theme incorporating many such themes. For example, in one study on cleanliness of body, food and water and home and village had sixteen messages (Singh, A. K. et al. 1991). The major topics covered by PHEI studies are: school health, child-care and child growth, nutrition and breast-feeding, immunisation, diarrhoea, coughs and colds, hygiene, cardio-vascular diseases, alcoholism, drugs and smoking, sexually transmitted diseases and AIDS. In addition, there are studies on health education which combine several topics. There are also a few reviews of Population-Health studies and critique of Population-Health Intervention Studies indicating these inadequacies.

In Ranchi, only three intervention studies have been noticed on PHL (Choudhary 1996; ICMR Project 1990; Naqvi 1996). The study conducted by ICMR (1990) was on cleanliness education. It used cleanliness education material for improving the knowledge, attitude and behaviour of the rural tribals of Ranchi district. The result shows significant difference in rural tribals with regard to their knowledge about cleanliness. In another attempt, Naqvi (1996) disseminated personal hygiene and environmental sanitation messages to educate the tribals in her study and the result was positive and satisfying. Choudhary (1996) studied the effect of Population-Health Education on the existing knowledge of tribal and non-tribal female college students. She used print materials, lectures and discussions for dissemination of the messages related to Population-Health Issues. She found that Population-Health Literacy levels were increased in the tribal and non-tribal female college students after Population-Health Education.

In addition to the studies reported above, we are also mentioning review of a few studies done in India and abroad. Salleras Samarti, et al. (1993) had compared the efficacy of three alternative health educational strategies on tuberculosis patients. The alternatives were (i) Education given at home by nursing personnel, (ii) Given on telephone by the same person and (iii) Given by the physician in his clinic. All the three strategies had produced better results compared to the Control Group, which had not received any instructions. But the most effective communication was the first strategy followed by the second. The Stanford five city projects had studied the effect of community health education on plasma cholesterol level and diet (Fortmann, S. et al. 1993a). After two years of health education, the increased nutritional knowledge among women had produced significant changes in dietary habits in the experimental condition, compared to control ones. Change in adult cigarette smoking prevalence after five years of community health education were also studied (Fortmann, S. et al. 1993b). The effectiveness of health education was evaluated by self-reporting, which was confirmed by examination of plasma thiocyanate and expired-air-carbon monoxide levels. Smoking prevalence over time decreased bad effects more in the Experimental Group than in the Control Groups.

In another study on cleanliness education of the tribals of south Bihar (now Jharkhand), educational materials were prepared on: (i) Cleanliness of body (ii) Cleanliness of food and water and (iii) Cleanliness of home and village. Fifty messages were incorporated in (i) Posters with coloured photographs taken in the field situation, and (ii) Coloured slides with synchronized commentary giving scientific explanation of health messages. Local Nagpuri language was used. Messages of each theme were summarized in a poem song in the manner of tribal dance song. The sample consisted of 250 cases in Control and 450 cases in Experimental Group. The intervention produced significant changes in some items due to poverty and deeply rooted cultural traditions (Singh, et al. 1991, 1995).

In Nepal, several methods of communications were used for providing knowledge on scientific intestinal worms. These were (i) Picture card games, (ii) Drama songs, (iii) Story-telling, (iv) Discussions and (v) A combination of all four. The last one was found to be the most effective method of communication. Women were more influenced than men. The sample consisted of 1393 villages (Akogun, 1992).

A "colostrums feeding education" was conducted by Tamagond and Saroja (1991). A random sample of 120 pregnant women with a minimum education of fifth standard and having at least one child and having not fed colostrums, were selected from the ante-natal clinics of hospital and nursing homes from the twin cities of Hubli and Dharwad in Karnataka state. The participants were selected with care and wisdom as the sample consisted of mothers with confirmed record of not feeding colostrums to their babies. The sample was divided into Control and Experimental Groups; the latter was further sub-divided into two on the basis of intervention methods used. Experimental Group 'A' was educated by three lectures using nine visual aids. Experimental Group 'B' was educated by three pamphlets with nine illustrations, mailed to them at weekly intervals. The mothers of Experimental Groups (53%) did feed colostrums either exclusively or with honey or boiled water, against none in the Control Group.

Granadillo, et al. (1994) conducted health education for mothers to influence their knowledge and attitudes to breast-feeding and immunization. The intervention group consisted of 20 mothers and the Control Group had 17 mothers. Monthly discussion meetings were held for seven months. In each meeting lectures were given and leaflets were distributed. Data was collected for experimental condition. In each meeting through a questionnaire, data was used with the Control Group. Eighty-five percent mothers of the Experimental Group gave correct answers compared to 37.5% mothers in the Control Groups.

George, et al. (1993) had conducted a research on health-nutrition education in twelve villages in Tamil Nadu, six of them served as Experimental Group with Growth Monitoring Package (GMP) and the other six served as Control Groups without GMP. About five hundred fifty children under the age of sixty months were studied for over four years. Anthropometric measures were taken after every four-five months. Comparisons between Control and Experimental Group children were done on monthly gains in height and weight, adjusted for age and sex. After thirty months of intervention there was no significant difference between Control and

Experimental Group villages. Growth Monitoring Package did not have any additional benefit and therefore it was integrated with child survival programme. A negative result in any research is as valuable as a positive one. But in the present research, the reasons for the failure of GMP has not been fully documented and argued, preventing one from learning important lessons from the non-verification of the main hypothesis of the research.

Sanchez, et al. (1991) evaluated the impact of health education on nutrition in eighty-eight families. The intervention was done by a group of nurses with diploma in health education by instructions on health and particularly on diet. Food consumption of the families was measured. The Experimental Group villagers were found to have higher levels of knowledge and more positive attitudes to proper diet than the Control Group villagers.

Ceratti, et al. (1990) had reported the results of "Nutrition education on obese students". The sample consisted of 12,354 students three to eighteen years of age. The intervention produced significant changes in the information level, attitudes and dietary habits.

Wilson, et al. (1991) studied "Knowledge about Faecal-Oral Route of Diarrhoea Transmission and Hand-washing Education" in sixty-five mothers in Indonesia. The scientific aetiology of diarrhoea was explained. The health messages were reinforced every fortnight. The intervention produced 89% reduction in diarrhoea episodes.

Odonsi and Ogan (1993) had educated school students and health-workers about three common intestinal nematode infections for 30 months. There was an average decrease of 78% to 86.9% in the prevalence of the three common intestinal infections.

Kumar, Kumar, and Raina (1989) have reported the study on the "Impact of Oral Rehydration Therapy on Maternal Beliefs and Practices" taking data from 69 villages in Haryana. Forty-seven villages served as Control Group. The programme was conducted by health workers and health volunteers. The impact was studied after two year of intervention. In the Experimental Group village 88.6% mothers used ORT compared with 22.8% in the Control Group villages. In the Experimental Group 68.3% mothers identified the symptoms and complications of diarrhoea compared to 32.8% in the Control Group village.

Rasheed (1993) has studied the perceptions of diarrhoeal diseases among mothers and mothers-to-be in Saudi Arabia. Knowledge of dehydration and malnutrition related complications were very low. Two-thirds of the educated sample accepted ORT as the best treatment of diarrhoea, whereas the less educated group preferred anti-diarrhoeal liquids and injections.

Hygiene is one important dimension of the present study. Many studies from 1982-98 have examined the effectiveness of intervention to change individual's behaviour related to dental health. The findings have shown that dental health education can result in improvements in objective measures of dental health behaviour and actual oral health measures. The studies have also shown that the interventions have only limited success in changing attitudes towards dental issues and lasts for a short period of time.

Pinfold (1990) conducted an intervention study to improve hand washing particularly before cooking, eating and after defecation, and also washing of dishes immediately after use. The study was conducted in rural Thailand in two groups. First group received verbal messages and the second group were given in addition to verbal messages, a plastic container with a tap to assist their activities. Expectedly, the intervention was more effective in the second group.

Aziz, et al. (1990) took rural samples in their studies and considered water, sanitation and general living under hygiene education in the children under five years age in two rural areas of Bangladesh. They had similar diarrhoeal morbidity rates found during 1990. The finding showed a reduction of 25% in the incidence of diarrhoea when the intervention was introduced.

The use and importance of clean water and sanitation was used as an intervention factor for a group of population in the study of Burundi. This intervention was used in the form of instructions at home and it continued for three months. It used audio visual materials. The result noted was that the intervention was very effective towards betterment.

Laiho, et al. (1993) had evaluated the effectiveness of "Three methods of oral health education in secondary schools" in Finland. These were (i) Lecture given by a dentist with the aid of transparencies and slides, (ii) Lecture given by peer group, consisting of six pupils from upper grades who used transparencies, extracts from video films and had a class room exhibition with pictures, slogans, dental aids and instruments, and (iii) Self-teaching was based on an exhibition from which the pupils searched for the information themselves. After the programmes, the pupil's opinion about the methods, their contents and implementation were obtained by a questionnaire which also obtained data on knowledge about certain oral health issues. The peer group oral health education got the highest ranking and the self-teaching the lowest.

Tooth-brushing habits of children and mother's assessment of dental health education were studied in Finland (Paunio, et al. 1994). The study investigated the reasons for poor tooth-brushing behaviour of three year old children and the relationship between mother's attitudes to dental education and the dental hygiene behaviour of the children. The data suggested the need for providing dental hygiene education to mothers, particularly from rural areas. The constant advice by the mother to the children regarding tooth brushing behaviour increased positively the behaviour pattern towards the issues related to dental phenomenon.

A comparison of dental health education in deprived and non-deprived schools of Edinburgh has been reported (Schou and Wight, 1994). A stratified random sample of 486 children was selected from 92 primary schools. Clinical examinations were done immediately before the beginning of the programme and one and four months after the programme. Tooth-brushes and take home materials were distributed to all children. Dental officers provided 20 minutes information session for each class and encouraged teachers to continue dental health activities within the class. The intervention produced significant changes. The improvements were more in non-deprived schools.

Naqvi (1996) studied on "Learning and Retention of personal hygiene and environmental sanitation education in the tribals". Out of one hundred and fifty tribal school students from grades 9 and 10, she divided equal number of boys and girls in her sample based on scientific method of sampling. The research design covered Control and Experimental Groups. The photographs and tape-recorded messages were used as intervention material. Although there was no significant difference in the impact of intervention among boys and girls, yet there was a significant increase in their behaviour due to interventions.

There are some intervention studies on coughs and colds and respiratory diseases which may be cited here.

Pandey, et al. (1990) used health workers to educate villagers in Kathmandu valley located about 24 km away from the city. The sample consisted of 1019 children under five years of age, who were followed for three years. The intervention consisted of education as well as health care services such as immunization and supply of medicines. The intervention produced 59% reduction in Acute Respiratory Infection (ARI) related death.

Bang, et al. (1990) conducted an intervention study in 58 villages as an Experimental Group covering 6,176 children aged up to four years. In the Control Group there were 44 villages with 3947 children. Children were given messages about childhood pneumonia including its management. The tradition birth attendants (dais) were trained to recognise childhood pneumonia and treat it. The intervention reduced the pneumonia-related deaths significantly in Experimental Group village.

Stergachis, et al. (1990) had studied the impact of mailed educational materials on self-care of Upper Respiratory Infection (URI). A group of 20,127 patients were assigned 22 panels of physicians. Patients were randomly assigned to Experimental (N=12,353) and Control (N=7,774) Groups. A four page educational material was sent to each patient by mail. In the Experimental Group there was a decrease in the visit to the medical centres for URI treatment by 14% more compared with Control Group patients.

The prevalence and treatment of acute respiratory infections in children aged four years was studied by Gunay, et al. (1994) by introducing intervention. The intervention group covered 69 children whereas Control Group consisted of 57 children. The intervention was made by educating the mothers regarding prevention and treatment of the diseases mentioned. The result showed that the number of children with infected diseases decreased towards going to clinics because of the intervention and the number of children of infected respiratory diseases did not show any improvement due to lack of intervention (Control Group).

Several studies on Population-Health Literacy programme have been reported and almost all the studies have shown positive and increasing improvements towards different dimensions of which some have been discussed earlier. The researcher feels that it is no use repeating different researches of the same nature yielding same result and attempt has been made here to indicate the researches done in different places by giving some references related to different dimensions of Population-Health Literacy under our study. This will help the other future researchers to use the materials for their references too.

In addition to the above referred studies, a number of other studies have also been reported in the other areas of Population-Health Literacy. Researchers have examined the role of *PHE Intervention effect in Child-Care and Child Growth literacy* (Allensworth 1994; Darby 1993; Hughes, et al. 1993; Jackson 1994; Williams, and Jones 1993; Berger, et al. 1994; Elder, et al. 1991; George, et al. 1993; Granadillo, et al. 1993; Pandey, et al. 1990; Rose 1994; Stregachis, et al. 1990); *Nutrition, Supplementary Food and Breast-Feeding Knowledge* (Aitken 1994; Ceratti, et al. 1990; Fortmann, et al. 1994; Levin-Zamir, et al. 1993; Sanchez, et al.

42

1991; Tamagond, and Saroja 1991); *Immunization* (Granadillo, et al. 1994); *Hygiene* (Brown 1994; Davies, and Croucher 1993; Dieleman, et al. 1994; Laiho, et al. 1993; Murthy, et al. 1990; Naqvi 1996; Paunio, et al. 1994; Pinfold 1990; Schou, and Wight 1994; Singh, Jayaswal, and Hans 1991); *Cough and Cold* (Bang, et al. 1990; Donham, et al. 1990; Elder, et al. 1991; Gunay, et al. 1994; Pandey, et al. 1990; Stergachis, et al. 1990); *Diarrhoea and ORT* (Akogun 1992; Kumar, Kumar and Raina 1989; Rasheed 1993; Wilson et al. 1991); *Respiratory Diseases* (Anderson, and Anderson 1994; Chen, Jr. et al. 1994; Kelder, et al. 1993; Lewis 1993; Schirm, et al. 1993); *Sexually Transmitted Diseases (STD) and AIDS* (Healton and Messeri 1993; Kelly, J. A. et al. 1993; Quirk, et al. 1993; Silvestre, A. J. 1994; Turner, J. C. et al. 1993; Wassif, O. M. et al. 1993); *Alcoholism and Drug* (Hillemand, B. 1993; Cayvelas, O. T. et al. 1993; Safer, L. A. and Harding, C. G. 1993; Witt, K. and Hector, O. 1991); *Smoking* (Fortmann, S. P. et al. 1993; Jeffery, R. W. et al. 1993; Kurtz, M. E. et al. 1990).

Almost all the studies mentioned above have accepted the positive role of intervention in enhancement of concerned literacy. Recently Baqui, et al. (2008) assessed the impact of an integrated nutrition and health programme on neonatal mortality in rural northern India in a study funded by USAID and through a grant from the Bill & Melinda Gates Foundation. Using a quasi-experimental design, we evaluated a programme facilitated by a nongovernmental organization that was implemented by the Indian government within existing infrastructure in two rural districts of Uttar Pradesh, Northern India. Mothers who had given birth in the 2 years preceding the surveys were interviewed during the baseline and end-line surveys. The primary outcome measure was reduction of neonatal mortality. In the intervention district, the frequency of home visits by community-based workers increased during both antenatal (from 16% to 56%) and postnatal (from 3% to 39%) periods, as did frequency of maternal and new-born care practices. In the control district, no improvement in home visits was observed and the only notable behaviour change was that women had saved money for emergency medical treatment. Neonatal mortality rates remained unchanged in both districts when only an antenatal visit was received. However, neonates who received a postnatal home visit within 28 days of birth had 34% lower neonatal mortality than those who received no postnatal visit.

Waddington et al. (2009) studied on Water, Sanitation and Hygiene interventions to combat childhood diarrhoea in developing countries like India and found that point-of-use water quality interventions appear to be highly effective – and indeed, more effective than water supply or source treatment in reducing diarrhoea in children. Hygiene interventions, particularly provision of soap for hand-washing, were found to be effective in reducing diarrhoea morbidity, and there was no evidence suggesting that compliance by those studies falls over time. The analysis suggested that sanitation 'hardware' interventions were also highly effective.

Patel et al. (2010) conducted a secondary data analysis of National Family Health Survey 2005-06 to estimate the infant and young child feeding indicators and determinants of poor feeding practices in India. They found that the rates of timely initiation of breastfeeding were higher among women who were better educated, were working, made more antenatal clinic visits, and were exposed to the radio. Similarly, the rates of timely complementary feeding were higher for mothers who had more antenatal visits and also for those who watched television. Higher numbers of antenatal care visits were associated with increased rates of exclusive breastfeeding.

JHARKHAND SCENARIO

Some of the interesting notes obtained from the official website of the Government of Jharkhand (2011) are of very important value to the present research.

Safe motherhood (SM)

In Jharkhand, majority of maternal deaths occur within 24 hours of childbirth. About one-quarter of maternal deaths take place during pregnancy and about 15% occur at the time of delivery. Four-fifths of maternal deaths are due to direct causes: such as haemorrhage, infection, complications related to unsafe abortion and hypertensive disorders. The remaining 20% are those aggravated by conditions such as malaria, anaemia or diabetes.

Breast-feeding (BF)

In Jharkhand, the median duration of breastfeeding is more than three years, but the median duration of exclusive breastfeeding is only 2-3 months contrary to the recommended six months. Only 26% of infants aged 6-9 months receive the recommended combination of breast milk and solid/mushy foods.

Immunization (IZ)/Vaccination

In Jharkhand, only 9% children aged 12-23 months are fully vaccinated as compared to the national average of 42%. Only 41 receive BCG, 22% all three doses of DPI, 31 % all three doses of polio, and only 18% receive the measles vaccine. The dropout rate from the first dose of DPI and polio to the third dose is as high as 50%. One-third of children of the state do not receive any vaccination.

Supplementary food (SF)

Malnutrition is the single most important risk factor for diseases. In Jharkhand, 54% children under age three are underweight, 49% are stunted, and 25% are wasted. The proportion experiencing malnutrition is higher in rural areas and among disadvantaged groups, particularly the scheduled tribes. The study based on the Body Mass Index, indicates that 41% women are undernourished and 73% women have some degree of anaemia. Only 56% of the households in Jharkhand use iodized salt at the recommended level.

Hygiene (HG)

In Jharkhand, only 14% of the births are institutional deliveries and another 17% receive assistance at the time of delivery from trained providers. Untrained traditional birth attendants attend two-thirds of deliveries. Many of the health institutions in Jharkhand do not have labour rooms, and many of the positions of female medical officers are vacant.

Diarrhoea (DR)

Diarrhoea is one of the most common illnesses among children. The development of oral therapy for the rehydration and treatment of children with dehydrating-diarrhoea has become the mainstay of the national diarrhoeal control programme. More recently, proper nutrition for children with diarrhoea is being viewed as an important adjunct to therapy, whereas antibiotics and other drugs play only a limited role. Intravenous therapy remains essential for diarrhoeal episodes associated with severe dehydration. In Jharkhand, 22% children suffer from diarrhoea at any given point of time and another 3% have diarrhoea with blood.

Cough and Cold (CC)

Acute Respiratory Infections (ARIs), mainly pneumonia, are a major cause of death and disability among children below five years of age. Approximately 30% of the ARI-related deaths are due to diseases preventable vaccines for measles, pertussis, and diphtheria while the remaining 70% of deaths are due to pneumonia. In Jharkhand, 22% of children below age three have ARIs and 28% suffer from fever.

Tripathy et al. (2010) conducted a cluster-randomised controlled trial on recent mothers in 36 clusters of Jharkhand and Orissa in a study funded by the Health Foundation, London, United Kingdom. Out of the 36 clusters, they assigned 18 clusters to intervention or control using stratified randomisation. Women were eligible to participate if they were aged 15–49 years, residing in the project area, and had given birth during the study. In intervention clusters, a facilitator convened 13 groups every month to support

48

participatory action and learning for women, and facilitated the development and implementation of strategies to address maternal and new-born health problems. The primary outcomes were reductions in neonatal mortality rate (NMR) by 32% in intervention clusters and a reduction of 57% in maternal depression scores in year 3 in the intervention clusters.

Gupta (2004), studied the recently completed Rapid Household Survey (RHS) under Reproductive Child Health (RCH) project which focussed on estimating indicators like the extent of Ante-Natal Care (ANC), institutional deliveries, safe deliveries, children's immunization coverage, contraceptive prevalence rate, unmet need etc. at district level of the new states and the parent states with changed territories. According to Gupta (2004), the need for the reliable demographic data for overall development planning in general and health and family welfare services in particular is unquestionable, especially, in the wake of urgent need to achieve the goal of population stabilization, when reproductive and child health services are revamped there is an urgent need of data on the status of reproductive and child health and utilization of the services, and hence his study is important. Some of the key findings based on the study of RCH of the newly formed states were that the reorganization of states not only made Jharkhand a relatively more urbanized and Bihar a high rural population station, but it also removed the imbalance in sex ratio in Jharkhand and worsening it even more in Bihar. Coming to other demographic indicators, the separation of Jharkhand from Bihar resulted in the change in the percentage of girls marrying below the age of 18. The early marriage age, particularly among the girls, to some extent has an impact on reproductive health of women. As per the survey, the percentage of girls marrying below the age of 18 was 58.2% in Bihar and slightly better at 50.8% in Jharkhand, but it was still alarmingly high when compared to other states. About the ante-natal care, the report highlighted that the coverage on ante-natal care was amongst the lowest in India, whereas that in Jharkhand was substantially higher than Bihar but still less than 50% coverage. Though in Jharkhand, the ANC coverage and the coverage of all ANC services was higher than that in Bihar, the extent of institutional deliveries (15%) and safe deliveries (20%) were same in both the states, much below the desired level. In both the states of Bihar and Jharkhand, the reported level of immunization was substantially low, as 53 and 34 percent of the children respectively did not receive any of the BCV, DPT, Polio and Measles vaccine. However the overall immunization coverage in Jharkhand was slightly better than Bihar. But when it comes to the other demographic indicator of family planning, compared to Bihar, in Jharkhand the reported level of knowledge of family planning was low.

Choudhary (2001) took a sample of tribal and non-tribal college students studying in Inter and Bachelor classes. Prior to the exposure of the Population-Health Education Materials (interventions) both the Control & Experimental Groups were measured on Population-Health Literacy Scale for benchmark data. After sometime the exposure of Population-Health Education materials was given only to the Experimental Group. After that both the groups were re-tested on Population-Health Literacy Scale. Thus a design of single group (before-after design) and double groups have been used. The results indicated low levels of Population-Health Literacy among all three groups. However, the role of intervention programme was significantly marked and significant differences were found in all ten dimensions of Population-Health Literacy Scale.

2.1 REVIEW OF LITERATURE: AN EVALUATION

Population-Health Education has become a central point of the studies of social and medical science. It is a key to the developmental agenda. As the literacy rate of the country increases, this area of study becomes more and more viable. PHE is directly related to the female literacy and health awareness. The issues related to family-planning, mother and child care, diet and nutrition, personal hygiene and environmental sanitation, physical and mental health and human organ donation are drawing utmost attention of the researchers. The Population-Health Education intervention has become a fruitful device to enhance the information about population and education. By giving intervention to change the attitudes of the woman towards above stated areas, the desired goal can be achieved to a great extent. The Population-Health Education intervention covers the topic like school-health, child-care and child-growth, nutrition and breast-feeding, immunization, diarrhoea, cough and cold, hygiene, cardiovascular diseases, alcoholism, drugs and smoking, sexually transmitted diseases and AIDS.

The studies related to the above topics have been the torch bearers of the problems related to Population-Health Education. Most of the studies cited in Review of Literature under Chapter 2 have been conducted in between 1985 and 1995. Since then a lot of water has flown from the Ganges. The female literacy rate of the country has increased dramatically, and so has the attitude towards Population-Health Education. The present study is a very small effort in changing the attitude towards Population-Health Education. The studies by Choudhary (1996), Gupta (2004), Baqui, Abdullah, et al. (2008), Waddington et al. (2009), Patel et al. (2010), provide a new dimension to the problem related to Population-Health Education. The National Health Report provides immense information related to Population-Health Education. The recent trends indicate that cardiovascular disease, tuberculosis, diabetes, high blood pressure, old age problems or gerontology, impotency are commonly found physical symptoms among the population. The problems such as depression, hyper-tension, stress, withdrawal, etc. are the most common psychological symptoms. However, these areas have not been properly covered in the study of Population-Health Education.

2.2   IMPORTANCE OF THE PRESENT STUDY

The review of literature has shown the importance of Population-Health Literacy for the people of India and Jharkhand in general and women in particular. Mothers are the first school for children. Health is one of the basic parts of one's life. A man without health cannot be thought to be perfect. He has to be mentally and physically sound. Mothers have the responsibility of bringing up their children. They have to take care of their children at every stage of life from conception to their maturity.

The proper diet during pregnancy, the diet of neonates and children at developing stages, the preventions pre and post pregnancy, the need for immunisation at early ages, and the knowledge about diseases of the children, are the basic education which every woman has to be aware of. This is the Population-Health Literacy.

Social scientists for the control of population as well as for the well-being of the children have to emphasize the need for the Population-Health Literacy and they have to trace out the factors associated with it as well as the ways of increasing the literacy among them.

All these concerns led the researcher to take such a problem for the present study and in light of the above facts the problem assumes a lot of significance.

The present study is different from the studies done earlier in the sense that the latter have not taken the educated housewives as the cases for their studies. It has been noted that uneducated housewives have significantly lower awareness about the health dimensions and they are almost equivalent to those housewives who have education below middle class.

CHAPTER 3

3 METHODOLOGY

3.1 AIMS

The study has been done to achieve the following aims:

1. To collect benchmark data from the educated (matriculation onwards) Hindu housewives of Ranchi regarding their knowledge about Population-Health issues

2. To conduct an intervention study using Population-Health Education of Hindu housewives of Ranchi

3. To examine the impact of age on Population-Health Literacy of Hindu housewives of Ranchi after intervention

3.2 HYPOTHESES

The following hypotheses were formulated for the study:

1. *The Population-Health Literacy will be low in the Hindu Housewives of Ranchi*

2. *The intervention (Population-Health Education) will increase the level of knowledge of Population-Health Literacy among Hindu Housewives of Ranchi*

3. *There will be no impact of age of Hindu Housewives of Ranchi on the* *intervention effect i.e. Population-Health Education*

3.3 SAMPLE

The sample comprised of 120 Hindu Housewives randomly selected from Ranchi, the capital city of Jharkhand. The age group of the sample ranged between 20 and 49 years. The sample was selected in two stages. Initially, Personal Data Sheet was applied among 500 Hindu Housewives to fetch their basic information such as name, age, profession, etc. Subsequently, 120 Hindu Housewives were selected on the basis of the classification of three age-groups consisting of 40 Hindu Housewives in each group. The categorisation of three age-groups is as follows:

The age of the first group of Hindu Housewives ranged between 20 and 29 years. The second age category ranged between 30 and 39 years and the third category ranged between 40 and 49 years. Each age-group consisted of 40 Hindu Housewives. All the three age-groups were again classified into two categories: Control Group and Experimental Group. Each sub-group consisted of 20 Hindu Housewives. The design of the research has been finalized on the basis of before and after design.

The data was collected in two stages. In the first stage, a benchmark data (Population-Health Literacy Questionnaire) was collected from all the 120 samples, which included both the Control and Experimental Groups. One week after collecting the benchmark data the intervention (Population-Health Education) was given only to the Experimental Groups and no information regarding the Population-Health Education was given to the Control Groups.

After three months from collecting the benchmark data from the entire 120 samples, the Population-Health Literacy Questionnaire was again applied to the Hindu Housewives of both Control and Experimental Groups (Table 3.1).

3.3.1   Inclusion Criteria for the Sample

a. Only Hindu Housewives of matriculation and above educational level were included

b. Age range between 20 to 49 years

c. Housewives of Ranchi town only

3.3.2   Exclusion Criteria

a.   No male sample was included

b.   No housewife other than Hindus

c.   Housewives below 20 years and above 49 years

d.   Housewives living outside Ranchi

Table - 3.1

SAMPLE-DESIGN

Age	N	Control Group					N	Experimental Group		
		Test I PHL Q	Intervention of PHE after Test I	Re-test PHL Q				Test I PHL Q	Intervention of PHE after Test I	Re-test PHL Q
40-49 years	20	Applied	No Intervention	Applied			20	Applied	Intervention	Applied
30-39 years	20	Applied	No Intervention	Applied			20	Applied	Intervention	Applied
20-29 years	20	Applied	No Intervention	Applied			20	Applied	Intervention	Applied
	60						60			

Total Sample = 120

PHL Q = Population-Health Literacy Questionnaire

PHE = Population-Health Education

3.4 TOOLS

The following tools were used to achieve the objectives under study:

3.4.1 Personal Data Questionnaire (PDQ)

The questionnaire consisted of personal data sheet. The items chosen were such so as to include the information needed for the research ahead such as identification of the household, number of other female members there, age marital status, etc. The educational level, occupation and income status of the husband were also required in the questionnaire (Appendix - I).

3.4.2   Population-Health Literacy questionnaire

The Population-Health Literacy Questionnaire developed by Choudhary and Singh (1994) was used to ascertain the Population-Health Literacy of the sample which covers ten main dimensions. The test has high level of reliability and validity. These dimensions in short are given below, which have been discussed in the previous chapter:

    a.   Adverse consequences of population explosion on quality of life (PEQ)

    b.   Timing of birth (TB)

    c.   Safe motherhood (SM)

    d.   Breast feeding (BF)

    e.   Immunization (IZ)/Vaccination

    f.   Supplementary food (SF)

    g.   Child growth (CG)

    h.   Hygiene (HG)

    i.   Diarrhoea (DR)

    j.   Cough and Cold (CC)

Each of the above mentioned dimensions covers 10 questions and therefore the questionnaire has 100 questions in all. Each question has three response alternatives and out of three only one response is correct. The range of score therefore is from 0 to 100. Correct response gets a score of one (Appendix – II).

3.4.3   Population-Health Educational Materials

The Population-Health Education Materials were used as intervention factors. The materials were related to all the ten dimensions of PHL issues. These test materials were meant for the Experimental Groups only. Some of the examples related to the above dimensions are given below for general information:

Adverse consequences of population explosion (PEQ)

- Use of condom/Nirodh and sterilization
- Concept of environment
- Concept of birth-rate
- Methods of birth spacing

Timing of Birth (TB)

- Years of birth spacing for sound health of mother and child
- Timing required by mother for recovery after pregnancy and child birth

Safe Motherhood (SM)

- Duration of labour pain after which hospitalization is necessary

- Consequences of severe vomiting during pregnancy

- Most dangerous pain during pregnancy

- Change of colour of eyelids

- Disease indicated by severe headache during pregnancy

Breast Feeding (BF)

- Substitute of breast milk

- Advantages of sufficient water content in mother's milk

- Breast feeding the child when mother is not seriously ill

- Preservation of breast milk at room temperature

- Duration and interval between two breast feedings

- Measures for getting sufficient breast milk

Immunization/Vaccination (IZ)

- Disease prevented by BCG vaccine

- Method of vaccination against polio

- Age of the child for DPT vaccine

- Age of child for BCG vaccination

- Interval between two doses of DPT

- Age of child for DPT vaccine

Supplementary Food (SF)

- Frequency of giving supplementary food to a child

- Consequence of child's food being cooked long before it is given to him/her

Child Growth (CG)

- Type of food material to be increased if the child is not gaining weight

- Weight gained during first three months after birth

- Type of vitamin lost due to diarrhoea or measles

- Frequency of feeding a child if he/she is not gaining weight

- Number of times a year a child of two years should be weighted

- Duration after which a child should be weighted from birth to one year of age

Hygiene (HG)

- Measures to be taken to clean water if it is not possible to boil it

- Frequency of washing the face of a child

- Health hazards due to faeces

Diarrhoea (DR)

- Prevention of diarrhoea

- Condition of fontanels in severe dehydration due to diarrhoea

- Preparation of ORS

- Types of liquid to be given to the child to replace loss of liquid

- Food/liquid to be given to a child unable to suck mother's breast

Cough and Cold (CC)

- How children suffering from coughs and colds should be made to rest?

- How do most coughs and colds, sore throats and runny nose get relieved?

- Place where coughs and colds spread rapidly

- Name of vitamin that prevents the child from pneumonia

- Measures taken to prevent the child from pneumonia

- When is the child suffering from coughs and colds at risk?

- Children more susceptible to pneumonia

Finally, the questionnaire contained 100 items and the range also varied from 0-100. The test had retest reliability of .58

with a validity of .36. The validity was determined by the method of statistical validity with a criterion of Choudhary and Singh (1994) who used females as subjects in their PHL study (Appendix – III).

3.5 PLAN OF ANALYSES

After collecting the data the following statistical techniques were used for analyses:

(i)   The percentages of correct responses have been calculated for getting an idea of the status of the initial knowledge of the urban housewives of both the Control and Experimental Groups

(ii)   The percentage has also been graphically represented in figures

(iii)   Mean scores and SDs have also been calculated for each of the three groups of both the Control and Experimental Groups. Further the significance of the mean-differences has been tested by t-tests, to examine the role of age as well as intervention

(iv)   Co-efficient of correlations has also been computed for obtaining the item-scale, scale-scale correlations for testing the validity of the PHL dimensions and scale

Chapter 4

4   ANALAYSIS AND DISCUSSION

The research has been done to relate education and age as two sociological variables with Population-Health Literacy. The first aim was to assess all the educated housewives on the level of Population-Health Literacy. The second aim was to introduce intervention as a psychological variable to determine its impact on the Population-Health Literacy. The third aim was to compare whether age-differences had any impact on the Population-Health Literacy of housewives by selecting housewives of three age-groups. The sample was divided into two equal groups: Control and Experimental Groups.

The study was conducted in two stages. At the first stage, i.e. prior to intervention, both the groups (Control and Experimental) had their PHL measured by applying PHL Questionnaire. In the second stage only Experimental Group was given intervention (PHEI). The Control Group was not introduced to any form of intervention. Subsequently both the groups were re-tested to determine the effect of intervention as per the experimental design.

A total number of 120 housewives belonging to Hindu community were selected for this purpose. Out of these 120 housewives, 60 housewives constituted Control Group while another 60 housewives formed Experimental Group. Both the Control and Experimental Groups were classified into three age-groups, each group represented 20 samples.

The knowledge concerning the Population-Health Issues have been measured by the Population-Health Literacy Questionnaire (PHL) framed and designed for measuring the knowledge concerning the issues related to the Population-Health. Population-Health Literacy Questionnaire (PHL) covered total ten themes, namely, Adverse consequences of Population Explosion on Quality of Life (PEQ), Timing of Birth (TB), Safe Motherhood (SM), Breast Feeding (BF) Immunization (1Z), Supplementary Food (SF), Child Growth (CG), Hygiene (HG), Diarrhoea (DR) and Cough and Cold (CC). Each of the themes was measured by ten items each and thus there were altogether hundred items.

The data obtained have been analysed by using suitable statistical techniques keeping in view the three aims of the present research and thereupon the hypotheses formulated on the basis of these aims.

The analysed data and discussions made upon these analyses have been reported under three heads:

(i) Status of Hindu Housewives (Control and Experimental Groups both) on Population-Health Literacy (PHL):

The analyses have been made keeping in view the first aim and hypothesis formulated thereupon. The analyses give a picture of the status of all Hindu Housewives based on Population-Health Literacy (PHL). The data was also considered as the benchmark data because it was collected prior to the introduction of the intervention (PHEI) materials.

(ii) Enhancement in Population-Health Literacy after intervention:

This analysis is based on the second aim of the research which tried to examine the effect of experimental variable on the sample. The Population-Health Education (PHE) materials as an intervention were introduced only to the Experimental Group. After introducing Population-Health Education (PHE) to the Experimental Group, the Population-Health Literacy (PHL) Questionnaire was again applied to them (Experimental Group). The data obtained after intervention from the Experimental Group was compared with the benchmark data of the same group. This procedure has tested the main hypothesis of the present research.

(iii) Age-difference in Population-Health Literacy (PHL):

This analysis of age-difference in Population-Health Literacy (PHL) is based on the third aim of the present research and the hypothesis made thereupon. The analysis tried to examine the effect of age-difference on experimental variable. After intervention to the Experimental Group, the comparison was made to see the effect of age-difference among the three Experimental Groups on PHE.

4.1 STATUS OF HINDU HOUSEWIVES (CONTROL AND EXPERIMENTAL GROUPS BOTH) ON POPULATION HEALTH LITERACY (PHL) (Benchmark Data)

The analyses have given a general idea of the Hindu Housewives on their knowledge about Population-Health related issues (PHL). The data have been analysed in two ways. The percentage of correct responses in each of the themes of PHL has been computed for the Control and Experimental Groups separately for each of the age-range sub-groups, and both the Control and Experimental Groups have been compared by using t-tests for determining the significances between their mean differences.

Analysed data have been presented in tabular forms. Table 4.1, 4.2, and 4.3 present the percentage of correct responses given by

68

the respondents of Control and Experimental Groups in the age range of 20-29, 30-39 and 40-49 years respectively before the application of intervention programme (pre-test). This is a bench mark data showing the awareness about PHL of both the Experimental and Control Groups.

Table 4.1

Percentage of correct Responses of Control and Experimental Groups (20-29 years) without intervention in PHL and its dimensions

Benchmark Data

S. No.	Dimensions of PHL	Control Group	Experimental Group	Difference in Percentage
1.	Adverse Consequences of Population Explosion on Quality of Life (PEQ)	20.00	23.3	3.3
2.	Timing of Birth (TB)	21.00	22.4	1.4
3.	Safe Motherhood (SM)	23.28	20.6	3.22
4.	Breast Feeding (BF)	20.8	22.00	1.2
5.	Immunization (IZ)	20.00	21.40	1.40

6.	Supplementary Food (SF)	22.50	19.40	3.10
7.	Child Growth (CG)	21.30	23.50	2.20
8.	Hygiene (HG)	19.50	23.40	3.90
9.	Diarrhoea (DR)	20.50	22.20	1.70
10.	Cough and Cold (CC)	21.20	22.40	1.20
Total	**Population-Health Literacy (PHL)**	**21.01**	**22.06**	**1.05**

N = 20 each in Control and Experimental Groups

Table 4.2

Percentage of correct Responses of Control and Experimental Groups (30-39 years) without intervention in PHL and its dimensions

Benchmark Data

S. No.	Dimensions of PHL	Control Group	Experimental Group	Difference in Percentage
1.	Adverse consequences of population Explosion on Quality of Life (PEQ)	46.7	48.3	1.6
2.	Timing of Birth (TB)	43	47	4

3.	Safe Motherhood (SM)	49	51	2
4.	Breast Feeding (BF)	43.2	52.6	9.4
5.	Immunization (IZ)	43.3	49.3	6
6.	Supplementary Food (SF)	44.2	53.7	9.5
7.	Child Growth (CG)	42.4	50.2	7.8
8.	Hygiene (HG)	44.3	48.2	3.9
9.	Diarrhoea (DR)	43.5	46.7	3.2
10.	Cough and Cold (CC)	43.10	45.20	2.10
Total	**Population-Health Literacy (PHL)**	**44.27**	**49.22**	**4.95**

N = 20 each in Control and Experimental Groups

Table 4.3

Percentage of correct Responses of Control and Experimental Groups (40-49 years) without intervention in PHL and its dimensions

Benchmark Data

S. No.	Dimensions of PHL	Control Group	Experimental Group	Difference in Percentage
1.	Adverse consequences of population Explosion on Quality of Life (PEQ)	33.3	28.00	5.3
2.	Timing of Birth (TB)	35.3	24.4	10.9
3.	Safe Motherhood (SM)	27.2	26.8	0.4
4.	Breast Feeding (BF)	35.3	27.8	7.5
5.	Immunization (IZ)	36.00	31.5	4.5
6.	Supplementary Food (SF)	33.3	26.7	6.6
7.	Child Growth (CG)	36.3	31.4	4.9
8.	Hygiene (HG)	36.2	23.9	12.3
9.	Diarrhoea (DR)	35.3	31.10	4.2
10.	Cough and Cold	35	26.90	8.10

72

	(CC)			
Total	Population-Health Literacy (PHL)	34.32	27.25	6.82

N = 20 each in Control and Experimental Groups

The analysed data gives the following result:

Adverse Consequences of Population Explosion on Quality of Life (PEQ)

The theme PEQ covers the questions on various aspects of Population Explosion such as knowledge of total population of India, causes of increasing population as well as their consequences, lack of food supply, increasing diseases, poor treatment, difficulty in the education etc. and spacing-problems etc. The percentage of correct responses shows the status of knowledge in the concerned theme.

Table 4.1 presents the percentage of correct responses in each of the themes of PHL and in total scale by the respondents of 20-29 years of age. The percentage of correct responses given by the Control Group is 20% and by the Experimental Group of is 23%, just a small difference of 3 percentage only. However both the groups have shown very poor knowledge in the theme of adverse consequences of Population Explosion on the quality of life.

However the Hindu Housewives in the age-range of 30-39 years have shown higher knowledge in relation to the adverse consequences of population explosion (PEQ) as depicted in Table 4.2. Both the groups have shown correct responses 46.7 (Control) and 48.3 (Experimental Group) in a difference of 1.6 percent only. This shows that the housewives of this age range have more correct information in PEQ than their counterparts (age range of 20-29 years). Further the housewives in the age-range of 40-49 years have shown poor knowledge in relation to PEQ theme. The Control Group has shown 33 percent of correct responses while the Experimental Group has shown 28 percent only as depicted in Table 4.3. The reason behind the greater level of awareness among the women in the age-group 30-39 was the effect of electronic media, level of marital affiliation and practical experiences put together.

Thus it can be concluded that the Hindu Housewives of the both lower age range (20-29 years) and higher age range (40-49 years) have low knowledge in relation to PEQ. However the housewives in the age range of 30-39 years are more matured to have more correct knowledge in PEQ.

Timing of Birth (TB)

The theme TB includes items relating time gap between two children, its uses for children as well as for mother and other issues related to pregnancy. The theme has been measured by 10 items.

Table 4.1 indicates poor knowledge of Hindu Housewives both of control (21%) and Experimental Groups (22.4%) in the age-range of 20-29 years in relation to TB. However the housewives in the age range of 30-39 years have shown higher knowledge in relation to TB, which is 43 percent and 47 percent respectively of Control and Experimental Groups. This has been shown in Table 4.2.

The housewives of higher (40-49 years) age range have again shown the poor knowledge in relation to TB. Control Group has given 35% correct responses while Experimental Group have given 24% correct responses in relation to Timing of Birth (TB), Control Group having more correct information concerning TB. (Table 4.3)

It has also been marked that the housewives belonging to 30-39 years age-range show more correct knowledge in relation to Timing of Birth (TB) compared to those who belonged to lower age-range as well higher age-range

Safe Motherhood (SM)

This theme is also measured by 10 items. The items are based on various issues related to the safety of motherhood, such as, labour pain, need of hospitalization, consequences of vomiting during pregnancy, diseases indicated during pregnancy etc.

Hindu Housewives of 20-29 years age-range have shown poor knowledge in relation to Safe Motherhood (SM) as depicted in Table 4.1 both the Control and Experimental Groups have almost equal position in their correct information.

Housewives of 30-39 years of age from both the Control and Experimental Groups have shown better knowledge in relation to safe motherhood (SM). The percentage of correct responses by the Control Group is 49 while it is 51 for the Experimental Group (Table 4.2) Again the housewives of higher age-range (40-49) have shown low knowledge in Safe Motherhood (SM). Both the Control Group (27%) and Experimental Group (26.8%) are on equal footings in the theme of SM (4.3).

Thus it can be concluded that only the status of fully matured housewives in age (30-39 years) have better knowledge of safe motherhood compared to their lower age or higher age counterpart groups.

Breast Feeding (BF)

Items of BF cover the knowledge concerning the breast milk, its substitute, properties, uses of breast feeding for lactating mother and duration of breast feeding etc.

Poor knowledge about breast feeding has been shown by both the Control and Experimental Groups in the 20-29 years of age-range as both of them have given 20.8% and 22% correct responses respectively (Table 4.1)

Control Group and Experimental Group of middle age-range (30-39 years) have shown 43.2% and 52.6% respectively in relation to breast feeding (BF) presented in Table 4.2.

The housewives in the age-range of 40-49 years have poor knowledge in Breast Feeding (BF) (Table 4.3).

Here the same trend has been marked as before that the Hindu Housewives of lower age-range and higher age-range have shown poor knowledge concerning BF, while the housewives (30-39 years) have shown higher knowledge in the theme of Breast Feeding (BF) of Population-Health Literacy (PHL).

Immunization (IZ)

This theme covers items related to various types of vaccinations, and immunization of children at different periods of life after birth for preventing them from the common diseases of children such as DPT, BCG, and Polio drops, etc.

Both the Control and Experimental Groups of first age-range 20-29 years have shown poor knowledge about Immunization

(IZ). Their percentages of correct responses are just 20% and 21.40% respectively (Table 4.1).

The housewives of second age-range (30-39 years) have shown much better knowledge in relation to Immunization. The percentages of correct responses are 43% and 49% respectively for Control and Experimental Groups (Table 4.2).

Again the housewives of elder age-range (40-49) have indicated poor response as far as the knowledge about Immunization was concerned (Table 4.3).

Thus like other themes the middle age-range (30-39) housewives have shown better knowledge in relation to Immunization in comparison to other two age-range groups. The trend has been the same for both the Control and Experimental Groups.

Supplementary Food (SF)

This theme of Supplementary Food covers the items seeking information about child's supplementary food as well as the frequency of feeding. The use of food cooked long before for the purpose of giving to the children and the quality of food, etc.

Both the groups, the Control as well as Experimental in the age-range of 20-29 years have shown poor knowledge in this item of SF (Table 4.1).

Better knowledge in these items has been shown by both the groups in the age-range of 30-39 years. Control Group have given 44% correct answer while the Experimental Group have given 53.7% correct answer (Table 4.2). The housewives in the age range of 40-49 years again have shown poor knowledge in relation to the items of Supplementary Food (Table 4.3).

Thus, it is here evident that again the middle age group have shown better knowledge in relation to SF as shown in other themes.

Child Growth (CG)

The Child Growth (CG), one of the themes of PHL covers 10 items. These items try to seek the information concerning the weight of child during birth, first three months of life, growth rate in different years, etc.

Both the Control as well as Experimental Groups have poor knowledge as these groups have given just 21% and 23.5% percent correct responses respectively in the age range of 20-29 years (Table 4.1).

The second age-range (30-39) group of housewives have shown better knowledge with respect to the items of Child Growth. The numbers of correct responses are 42.4% and 50.2% respectively for Control and Experimental Groups (Table 4.2)

Control Group in the 40-49 years age-range has given slightly better correct responses (36%) compared to that of Experimental Group (31%) in the same age-range. But both the percentages are below average (Table 4.3). Thus the matured adult housewives have better knowledge of Child Growth than lower and higher age-range housewives.

Hygiene (HG)

The theme Hygiene (HG) covers the items to test the knowledge of respondents about the hygiene of the children about keeping them clean, bathing, washing, cleaning the faeces, etc.

The knowledge shown both by the Control as well as the Experimental Group is poor, i.e. 20 and 23 percent respectively, in 20-29 years age-group (Table 4.1).

But the second age-range group (30-39 years) housewives have shown better knowledge in relation to Hygiene. The housewives of Control and Experimental Groups have given 44 and 48 percent correct answers respectively (Table 4.2).

Control Group in 40-49 years age-range has shown a bit higher knowledge (36%) as compared to that (24%) of Experimental Group (Table 4.3).

The conclusion is drawn that the Hindu Housewives have poor knowledge in relation to Hygiene. Only the housewives in the age-range of 30-39 have a little better knowledge in relation to their other counterparts.

Diarrhoea (DR)

This theme also includes 10 items. The items cover the questions related to the symptoms of Diarrhoea, dehydration and Oral rehydration solution, and consequences in children, etc.

The housewives in the range of 20-29 years have shown poor knowledge in the items of Diarrhoea (DR). The percentage of Control Group (21%) and that of Experimental Group (22%) are shown in Table 4.1. The housewives in the age-range of 30-39 years have shown much better knowledge in the items of Diarrhoea (DR). The percentage of their correct answers are 44% and 47% respectively for Control and Experimental Groups, (Table 4.2) Again the housewives in the age-range of 40-49 years have indicated poor knowledge as depicted in Table 4.3. The Control Group has shown better knowledge of 35 percent compared to 27 percent by the Experimental Group.

Thus, like other themes the housewives of 30-39 years age-range have given more correct responses than that of high and low age-groups.

Cough and Cold (CC)

Cough and Cold (CC) as one of the themes of PHL is also measured by its 10 items which test the knowledge about children's cough and cold, prevention for children suffering from Cough and Cold, susceptibility to Pneumonia, use of drugs and vitamins to save from Pneumonia etc.

The housewives in the age-range of 20-29 years have shown poor knowledge concerning the items of Cough and Cold. The percentages of correct responses are 21% and 22% respectively for the Control and Experimental Groups (Table 4.1)

As for the other themes the house-wives in the age-range of 30-39 years have shown better knowledge. The percentages of their correct responses are 43% and 45% respectively for the Control and the Experimental Groups (Table 4.2)

The housewives in the age-range of 40-49 years of Control Group have shown better knowledge (35%) compared to their counterparts (27%) as shown in Table 4.3.

Thus in relation to the theme of Cough and Cold (CC) the Hindu Housewives have shown poor knowledge except to those housewives who belonged to 30-39 years age-group. The trend of knowledge is almost equal in both the Control and Experimental Groups of the three different age-groups.

The status of Hindu Housewives of both the Control and Experimental Groups belonging to three age-level groups has already been discussed above. In each of the 10 themes of PHL the Hindu Housewives of both the Control and Experimental Groups of 20-29, and 40-49 years age-range have shown poor knowledge in relation to the concerned themes. However in all these themes the housewives belonging to 30-39 years age-group have shown better knowledge in relation to the asked items.

The three tables (4.1, 4.2, and 4.3) presented earlier as benchmark data have already been discussed with the percentage of correct answers in Population-Health Literacy (PHL).

Population-Health Literacy (PHL): All Themes

PHL consists of 10 themes, each theme measured by 10 items making a total of 100 items in the PHL Questionnaire. The percentage of correct responses in relation to PHL have also been computed and presented in the Tables discussed above.

Table 4.1 depicts that both of the Control and Experimental Groups of 20-29 years give correct responses of 21 and 22 percent respectively. Again, as per the trend in all the themes of PHL the housewives of 30-39 years age-range have shown higher knowledge in PHL compared to other two age-groups. This trend is seen in both the Control and Experimental Groups who have given 43 and 45 percents correct responses, as depicted in Table 4.2.

Table 4.3 shows that the housewives in the 40-49 years age range again have shown poor knowledge in PHL. Control Group has shown better correct responses (34%) than Experimental Group (27%). However both the lesser and higher age-group housewives have lesser knowledge in PHL compared to the Hindu Housewives of 30-39 yeas age-range. However in total their knowledge is below the average.

This shows that the Hindu Housewives are devoid of proper correct knowledge in relation to various issues of Population-Health Literacy (PHL).

Tables: 4.1 to 4.3 discussed above have also been graphically represented in Figures: 4.1 and 4.2.

84

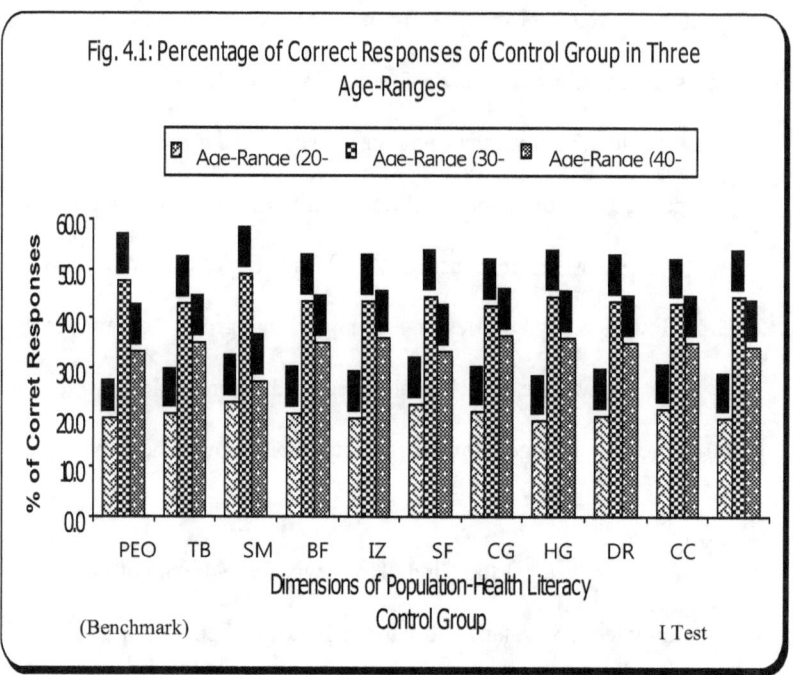

Fig. 4.1: Percentage of Correct Responses of Control Group in Three Age-Ranges

PEQ = Adverse consequence of Population Explosion on Quality of life	TB = Timing of Birth
SM = Safe Motherhood	BF = Breast Feeding
IZ = Immunization	SF = Supplementary Food
CG = Child Growth	HG = Hygiene
DR = Diarrhoea	CC = Cough and Cold
TPHL = Total Population-Health Literacy	

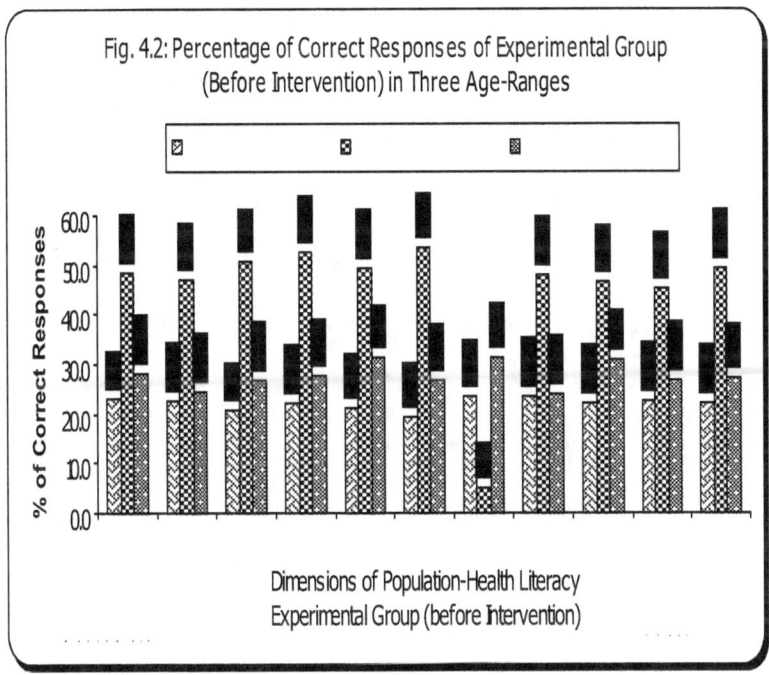

Fig. 4.2: Percentage of Correct Responses of Experimental Group (Before Intervention) in Three Age-Ranges

PEQ = Adverse consequence of Population Explosion on Quality of life	TB = Timing of Birth
SM = Safe Motherhood	BF = Breast Feeding
IZ = Immunization	SF = Supplementary Food
CG = Child Growth	HG = Hygiene
DR = Diarrhoea	CC = Cough and Cold
TPHL = Total Population-Health Literacy	

An analytical view of the Figures 4.1 and 4.2 reveal the following facts:

(i)   The Control Group in the age-range of 20-29 years has shown very poor knowledge in all the themes of PHL.

Similar trend has been marked in the Experimental Group of the same age-range. The percentage of correct responses is low, in both the groups (less than 25%). The same point is marked in the case of total scale of PHL.

(ii)   The magnitude of difference between Control and Experimental Group is also very low. Both have poor knowledge.

(iii)   The Control Group in the age-range of 30-39 years has shown better knowledge, though it is less than 50 percent but much above 25%. The Experimental Group has also shown the similar trend in all the themes of PHL as well as in total scale. In one or two cases it is just above 50% in giving correct responses.

(iv)   However the magnitude of difference between Control and Experimental Group is not too high. This indicates that both the groups have almost same degree of knowledge in relation to the themes of PHL as well as in total PHL.

(v)   The Control Group in the age-range of 40-49 years have again shown poor knowledge in relation to all the themes of PHL as well as in total PHL. Similar trend has also been depicted by the Experimental Group.

(vi)   Both the Control and Experimental Groups do not differ much in the magnitude. Both seem to be on equal status in knowledge about the themes of PHL.

TESTING THE EQUALITY OF STATUS OF CONTROL AND EXPERIMENTAL GROUPS BEFORE INTERVENTION

Prior to applying the intervention programme in Experimental Group it is experimentally needed to match both of the groups in initial Population-Health Literacy (PHL) or in other words it is must to keep both the groups in equal status in PHL. Before intervention both the groups have been analysed and both the groups have been tried to match with each other in PHL. Two methods have been applied to match them. Percentage of correct respondents has been calculated for the total sample in PHL as well as its ten dimensions. Further the t-ratio between Control Group and Experimental Group have been calculated to examine the mean differences between the aforesaid groups.

The percentages of correct responses of Control and Experimental Groups (total) sample in PHL and its dimensions prior to intervention have been given in Table 4.4.

It is marked in the Table that the percentage of correct response in both the groups are almost equal. Control Group differs from experimenting group in low magnitude. The maximum difference between these groups is of 1.83 percent in relation to Timing of Birth (TB) dimension followed by Child Growth (CG) of 1.73 percent. The minimum difference of 0.03% is seen in relation to the area of Supplementary Food (SF) dimension. In Population-Health Literacy (PHL) both groups differ by 0.36% only, a quite negligible difference.

The percentages of correct responses given in above Table have also been graphically represented in Figure 4.3. The figure clearly shows that the bars representing the Control and Experimental Groups are almost equal or slightly different (above or below) to each other. This clearly shows that both the groups do not differ in their levels of Population-Health Literacy (PHL). This trend can be seen in each of the dimensions of PHL also.

Thus it is marked here that both the Control and Experimental Groups are matched as far as the percentage of correct responses are concerned.

Further the significances of mean differences between Control and Experimental Groups have also been tested by t-tests. The application of t-tests has been made separately for each of the three age-level sub-groups, namely 20-29, 30-39, and 40-49 years.

Table 4.4

Percentage of correct responses of Control and Experimental Groups (Total Sample) without intervention in PHL and its dimensions

Benchmark Data

S. No.	Dimensions of PHL	Control Group	Experimental Group	Difference in Percentage
1.	Adverse consequences of population Explosion on Quality of Life (PEQ)	33.3	33.2	0.1
2.	Timing of Birth (TB)	33.1	31.27	1.83
3.	Safe Motherhood (SM)	33.16	32.80	0.36
4.	Breast Feeding (BF)	33.1	34.13	1.12
5.	Immunization (IZ)	33.1	34.07	1.03
6.	Supplementary Food (SF)	33.3	33.27	0.03
7.	Child Growth (CG)	33.3	35.03	1.73
8.	Hygiene (HG)	33.3	31.83	1.47
9.	Diarrhoea (DR)	33.1	33.3	0.2
10.	Cough and Cold (CC)	33.1	31.15	1.5

Tot al	Population-Health Literacy (PHL)	33.2	32.84	0.36

N = 60 each in Control and Experimental Groups

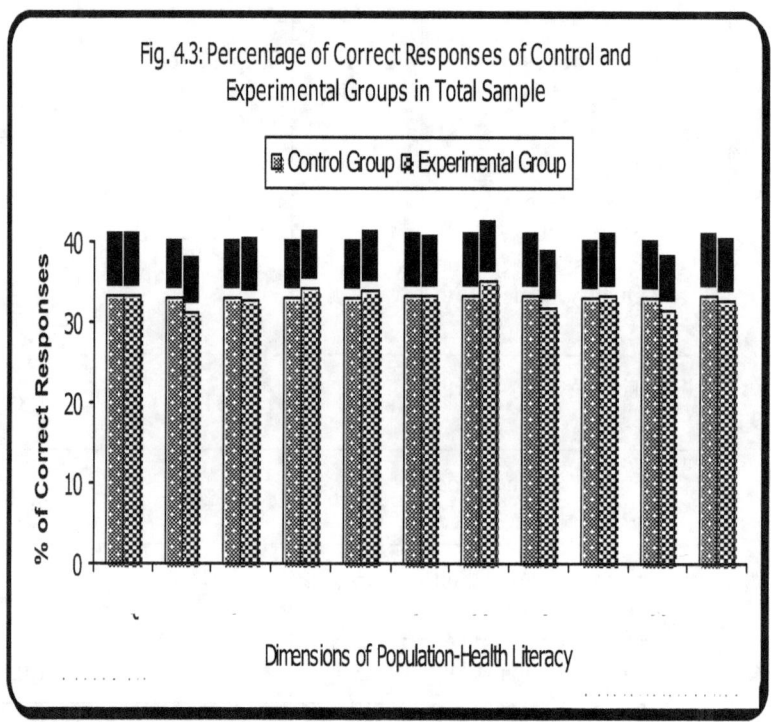

Fig. 4.3: Percentage of Correct Responses of Control and Experimental Groups in Total Sample

PEQ = Adverse consequence of Population Explosion on Quality of life	TB = Timing of Birth
SM = Safe Motherhood	BF = Breast Feeding
IZ = Immunization	SF = Supplementary Food
CG = Child Growth	HG = Hygiene
DR = Diarrhoea	CC = Cough and Cold
TPHL = Total Population-Health Literacy	

Table 4.5 presents the comparisons of Control and Experimental Groups in 20-29 years age-group. The comparisons have been made in relation to all the ten dimensions of PHL as well as in PHL. Thus there are eleven t-ratios. Out of these t-values no t-value is statistically significant. This shows that Control Group and Experimental Group do not differ significantly in any dimension of PHL. These groups also do not differ with each other in total PHL. The trend of t-values has clearly indicated that both the groups are equal in footing. Any of the two groups can be used as Experimental Group.

Table 4.6 presents the comparisons of Control and Experimental Groups of 30-39 years in all the ten dimensions of Population-Health Literacy (PHL) and total scale of PHL.

We observe the same trend as found above. Out of eleven t-values no one was statistically significant. This again suggests that Control and Experimental Groups are alike and have equal status as far as the Population-Health Literacy knowledge is concerned.

Table 4.7 presents the comparisons of Control and Experimental Groups of 40-49 years age-groups in Population-Health Literacy (PHL) and its dimensions. As previous Tables here again the control and the Experimental Groups have been compared

in eleven dimensions as well as in PHL.

Table 4.5

Comparisons of Control and Experimental Groups (20-29 Years) in
PHL and its dimensions

Benchmark Data

S. No.	Dimensions of PHL	Control Group		Experimental Group		t-values
		M	SD	M	SD	
1.	Adverse consequences of Population Explosion on Quality of Life (PEQ)	4.50	3.15	4.80	2.65	0.33
2.	Timing of Birth (TB)	4.20	3.25	4.50	2.70	0.32
3.	Safe Motherhood (SM)	3.90	3.65	3.40	3.15	0.23
4.	Breast Feeding (BF)	3.60	3.10	3.90	3.30	0.29
5.	Immunization (IZ)	4.00	2.90	4.20	3.55	0.19
6.	Supplementary Food (SF)	3.80	3.05	4.05	3.74	0.69
7.	Child Growth (CG)	3.20	2.80	4.70	3.34	1.55
8.	Hygiene (HG)	4.10	2.65	3.65	3.19	0.49

9.	Diarrhoea	4.60	3.06	5.10	3.05	0.53
10.	Cold & Cough (CC)	4.80	3.15	5.10	3.34	0.30
Total	**Population-Health Literacy (PHL)**	**40.70**	**14.07**	**45.40**	**15.66**	**0.57**

All t-values are statistically insignificant

N = 20 each in Control and Experimental Groups

Table 4.6

Comparisons of Control and Experimental Groups (30-39 Years) in PHL and its dimensions

Benchmark Data

S. No.	Dimensions of PHL	Control Group		Experimental Group		t-values
		M	**SD**	**M**	**SD**	
1.	Adverse consequences of Population Explosion on Quality of Life (PEQ)	6.15	3.65	6.70	3.62	0.48
2.	Timing of Birth (TB)	4.70	3.15	5.40	3.56	0.66
3.	Safe Motherhood (SM)	5.90	4.10	6.35	4.13	0.35
4.	Breast Feeding (BF)	5.30	3.85	5.95	3.72	0.54

5.	Immunization (IZ)	5.50	3.75	6.40	4.11	0.73
6.	Supplementary Food (SF)	6.80	4.32	6.70	3.66	0.08
7.	Child Growth (CG)	6.70	4.14	5.30	4.03	1.09
8.	Hygiene (HG)	6.10	3.90	6.65	3.55	0.47
9.	Diarrhoea	5.65	3.70	5.85	4.14	0.16
10.	Cold & Cough (CC)	5.70	4.15	6.80	3.72	0.89
Total	**Population-Health Literacy (PHL)**	**58.50**	**17.04**	**62.10**	**18.20**	**0.65**

All t-values are statistically insignificant

N = 20 each in Control and Experimental Groups

Table 4.7

Comparisons of Control and Experimental Groups (40-49 Years) in PHL and its dimensions

Benchmark Data

S. No.	Dimensions of PHL	Control Group		Experimental Group		t-values
		M	SD	M	SD	
1.	Adverse consequences of Population Explosion on Quality of Life	5.15	4.10	5.95	4.37	0.60

	(PEQ)					
2.	Timing of Birth (TB)	5.45	3.91	6.10	4.05	0.52
3.	Safe Motherhood (SM)	4.85	3.81	5.30	4.92	0.32
4.	Breast Feeding (BF)	5.25	4.05	6.75	4.22	1.15
5.	Immunization (IZ)	6.10	3.75	4.80	4.15	1.04
6.	Supplementary Food (SF)	5.55	3.19	5.90	3.63	0.32
7.	Child Growth (CG)	4.90	4.17	6.30	4.25	1.06
8.	Hygiene (HG)	5.30	3.65	6.10	3.91	0.65
9.	Diarrhoea	6.15	4.16	5.05	4.29	0.82
10.	Cold & Cough (CC)	6.10	3.27	6.50	3.65	0.36
Total	**Population-Health Literacy (PHL)**	**54.65**	**19.91**	**58.85**	**17.38**	**0.71**

All t-values are statistically insignificant

N = 20 each in Control and Experimental Groups

96

All the t-values are statistically insignificant. Here again it has been proved that Control and Experimental Groups do not differ with each other in any dimensions of PHL or in total scores.

Table 4.8 has compared the Control and Experimental Groups (total sample) in Population-Health Literacy. The t-value indicates that both the groups do not differ significantly. This indication also supports the findings reported above.

Table 4.8

Comparisons of Control and Experimental Groups (Total Sample) without
Intervention in Population-Health Literacy (PHL)

Benchmark Data

S. No.	Dimensions	Control Group		Experimental Group		t-values
		M	SD	M	SD	
1.	Population-Health Literacy (PHL)	51.28	18.94	55.45	19.55	1.19[NS]

NS = Not Significant

N = 60 each in Control and Experimental Groups

The trend observed in all the previous four Tables clearly indicates that both the groups are well matched in initial knowledge (bench mark data before intervention) of PHL and any of the two groups can be used as an Experimental Group.

TESTING THE FIRST HYPOTHESIS

The first aim of the research was to conduct a basic survey to collect a benchmark data of the educated (matriculation onwards) Hindu Housewives of Ranchi town on their knowledge about Population-Health Issues. Based on this aim the first hypothesis reads as:

"The Population-Health Literacy will be low in the Hindu Housewives of Ranchi"

The analysed data have been presented in Tables 4.1 to 4.3 and Figures 4.1 and 4.2. The tables present the percentage of correct responses of Hindu Housewives of both the Control and Experimental Groups prior to the exposure of experimental variable, namely, Population-Health Education (PHE) materials. The percentages have also been graphically represented in two figures. The percentages have been computed for all the three age-groups separately and for all the ten themes of Population-Health Literacy (PHL) and for the total PHL.

Further the percentage of total cases of Control Group and Experimental Group have also been computed separately (Table 4.4) and graphically represented (Figure 4.3). The mean scores of both the groups have also been calculated separately and compared by using t-tests (Tables 4.5 to 4.8). The analysed data have clearly shown that both the groups have very poor knowledge though the subjects of both the groups are educated. This shows that the general education does not give knowledge about Population-Health Issues. The trend has been marked similar for all the dimensions of Population-Health Literacy (PHL) namely, PEQ, TB, SM, BF, IZ, SF, CG, HG, DR, and CC.

Hindu Housewives belonging to age group 20-29 years have shown poorest knowledge concerning PHL. In most of the cases they have given correct answers in lesser than 25%. However the Hindu Housewives of 30-39 years age have been shown a slightly higher literacy above 40% correct responses but less than 50% correct responses. The housewives belonging to 40-49 years age group have shown higher knowledge than the 20-29 years age group but have lower knowledge as compared to 30-39 years age group counterparts. In most of the cases it is less than 30% correct responses.

Further the comparisons of mean scores have shown that prior to intervention both the groups neither differ significantly in any dimension of PHL nor in total PHL. All groups stand equal and show poor knowledge. It has been apparent from the analyses that the Hindu Housewives, though literate, have poor knowledge as far as their Population-Health Literacy issues are concerned.

Therefore, the present hypothesis has been supported.

USE OF INTERVENTION MATERIALS

After matching both the Control and Experimental Groups in the levels of Population-Health Literacy, based on ten dimensions it was decided to expose the Intervention Materials to the Experimental Group only.

POPULATION-HEALTH EDUCATION MATERIALS

During intervention programme the Population-Health Education Materials were exposed to the urban housewives of Experimental Group only. The details of Population-Health Education Materials have already been given in Chapter-3 on Methodology. The materials used as the intervening materials are concerned with all the ten dimensions of Population-Health Literacy Scale, namely, Adverse Consequences of Population Explosion (PEQ), Timing of Birth (TB), Safe Motherhood (SM), Breast Feeding (BE), Immunization (IZ), Supplementary Food (SF), Child Growth (CG), Hygiene (HG), Diarrhoea (DR), and Cough and Cold(CC).

Concerning the above dimensions of PHL the intervention materials consists of slogans/statements to be lectured and discussed with the respondents so that their knowledge concerning Population-Health Issues be enhanced for better motherhood.   As   mentioned earlier, the Experimental Group consisted of three sub-groups based on different age-range, namely, 20-29 years, 30-39 years and 40-49 years housewives of urban area. The intervention programme has been introduced to all the three sub-groups. Each sub-group consisted of 20 housewives.

Intervention was exposed through lectures and discussions. Messages and slogans used in Population-Health Education Materials were put before them and discussed so that their knowledge about Population-Health Issues is enhanced.

This was the procedure which took about three months in finishing the programme in each of the housewives of the said sub-groups between the data obtained on two occasions.

4.2 ENHANCEMENT IN POPULATION-HEALTH LITERACY AFTER INTERVENTION

Does the intervention increase the Population-Health Literacy in the housewives of Experimental Group?

The question above noted is the main theme of the present research work. As explained in the methodology the objectives of the present research are to assess the status of urban housewives in Population-Health Literacy (PHL) and then to examine the role of intervention of Population-Health knowledge in Experimental Group.

After the exposure of PHE (Population-Health Education) materials the Experimental Group has been re-tested in PHL (Population-Health Literacy). The data taken before and after intervention has been compared and analysed to examine the role of intervention as well as the differences between the data obtained in two occasions. To examine the role of intervention programme in the Experimental Group, two techniques have been used. First the status of Control and Experimental Groups has been ascertained before any intervention. The status of urban housewives have been assessed by calculating the percentage of correct responses given in each of the dimension of PHL as well as their total scores and further both the Control and Experimental Groups have been compared by t-tests to ascertain that both the groups do not differ with each other in the PHL status. After knowing the status of both the groups the intervention was introduced to the Experimental Group only and retest on PHL was applied. The first test data (before intervention) and re-test data (after intervention) have been compared in two ways. First taking the total sample, their status on PHL before and after interventions has been compared and then the Control and Experimental Groups in each of the three age-range groups have been compared by t-tests.

Let the role of intervention be confirmed

Table 4.9 presents the percentage of correct responses of Experimental Group (20-29 years age-group) in before and after-test conditions, in the dimensions of Population-Health Literacy. The percentage of Experimental Group before intervention is 23.3, while it goes to 40.7% after intervention making an enhancement of 17.4% knowledge after invention in relation to Adverse Consequences of Population Explosion on Quality of Life (PEQ). In relation to Timing of Birth (TB) there is an enhancement of 19.9% in knowledge after intervention. In the dimension of safe motherhood prior to the intervention the Experimental Group has shown 20.6% of correct responses whereas after intervention the same group enhanced the number of correct responses (38.15%), an enhancement of 17.55%. Similarly there is an enhancement of 17.30% in the knowledge of Breast Feeding (BF) after intervention. In the dimension of immunization (IZ) after intervention the Experimental Group shows 19.10% enhancement in the knowledge. In the next dimension of supplementary food (SF) the Experimental Group has given 19.40% correct responses before intervention while the percentage of correct responses rises up to 37.10% after intervention. Thus there is an increase of 17.70% in the knowledge of PHL. The Experimental Group has shown an enhancement of

21.50% after intervention in the Child Growth (CG) dimension of PHL. In the dimension of hygiene (HG) the difference between before and after interventions in the knowledge is of 23.70%. In the last two dimensions of Diarrhoea (DR) and Cough and Cold (CC) the Experimental Group has shown the percentage of 22.20% and 22.40% correct responses respectively before intervention. When the group was given intervention, the percentage rose to 48.6% and 46.55% respectively. In total PHL scale the difference between before and after intervention measures was 18.49%.

Table 4.9

Percentage of correct Responses of Experimental Group in Before and After Interventions of 20-29 years age-group in PHL and its dimensions

S. No.	Dimensions of PHL	Experimental Group		
		Before Intervention	**After Intervention**	**Gain in %**
1.	Adverse Consequences of Population Explosion on Quality of Life (PEQ)	23.3	40.7	17.4
2.	Timing of Birth (TB)	22.4	42.3	19.9
3.	Safe Motherhood (SM)	20.6	38.15	17.55

4.	Breast Feeding (BF)	22.00	39.30	17.30
5.	Immunization (IZ)	21.40	40.5	19.10
6.	Supplementary Food (SF)	19.40	37.10	17.70
7.	Child Growth (CG)	23.50	45.00	21.50
8.	Hygiene (HG)	23.40	47.10	23.70
9.	Diarrhoea (DR)	22.20	48.60	26.40
10.	Cough and Cold (CC)	22.40	46.55	24.15
Total	**Population-Health Literacy (PHL)**	**22.06**	**40.55**	**18.49**

N=20

All these findings reveal that the urban housewives have shown marked differences in their knowledge of PHL and its dimensions after interventions. The percentages have risen significantly after intervention. It has a positive effect on their knowledge. The percentages of 'before and after measures of PHL knowledge' have been presented in Table 4.9 and Figure 4.4.

The results have clearly indicated that the Experimental Group has a big gain in PHL. Now the question arises whether this enhancement in Experimental Group of 20-29 years age in PHL knowledge is statistically significant or not. The mean scores and SDs of the two Experimental conditions have also been computed for measuring the significance, between mean differences of before-after intervention measures.

Table 4.10 presents the comparisons of the measures of Experimental Group in before and after intervention conditions in PHL and all its dimensions. There are eleven t-values testing the significance of mean differences. Out of these eleven t-values, only two t-values are not statistically significant, namely, in relation to Child Growth (CG) and Cold and cough (CC) dimensions of PHL, though in both the cases the mean scores are greater in the case of after intervention measures compared to before intervention measures. In remaining nine other comparisons the t-values are statistically significant. This clearly indicates that intervention has a significant role in the enhancement of knowledge of urban housewives. The mean scores of after intervention measures are significantly greater than those of before intervention measures. This table has confirmed the significant role of intervention in Experimental Group in the age-range of 20-29 years.

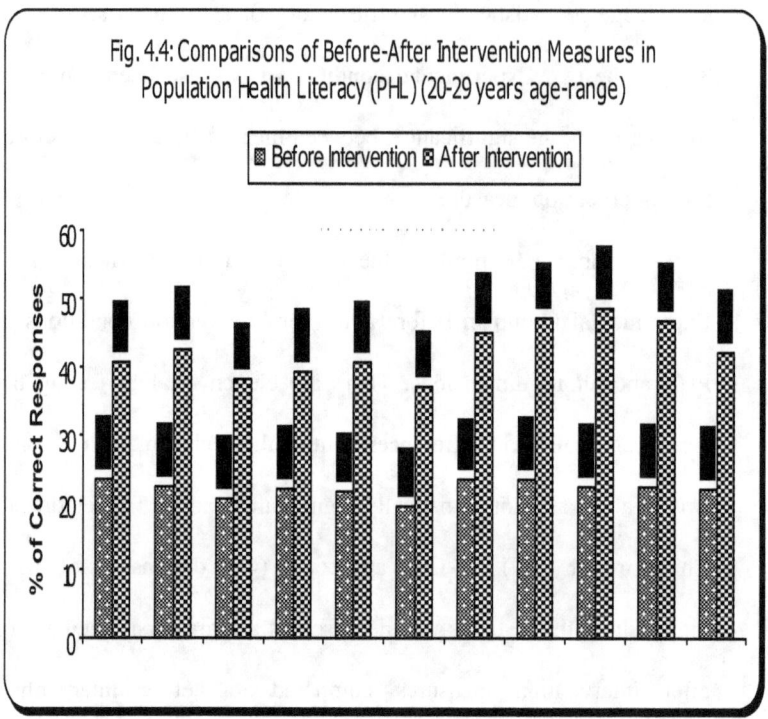

Fig. 4.4: Comparisons of Before-After Intervention Measures in Population Health Literacy (PHL) (20-29 years age-range)

PEQ = Adverse consequence of Population Explosion on Quality of life	TB = Timing of Birth
SM = Safe Motherhood	BF = Breast Feeding
IZ = Immunization	SF = Supplementary Food
CG = Child Growth	HG = Hygiene
DR = Diarrhoea	CC = Cough and Cold
TPHL = Total Population-Health Literacy	

Table 4.10

Comparisons of Experimental Groups (20-29 years) in Before and After intervention conditions in PHL and its dimensions

S. No.	Dimensions of PHL	Experimental Group				t-values
		Before Intervention		After Intervention		
		M	SD	M	SD	
1.	Adverse consequences of Population Explosion on Quality of Life (PEQ)	4.80	2.63	7.25	3.71	2.40*
2.	Timing of Birth (TB)	4.50	2.70	6.95	4.12	2.23*
3.	Safe Motherhood (SM)	3.40	3.15	6.30	3.65	2.69**
4.	Breast Feeding (BF)	3.90	3.30	6.80	4.20	2.44*
5.	Immunization (IZ)	4.20	3.55	7.60	3.80	2.93**
6.	Supplementary Food (SF)	4.05	3.74	6.75	4.50	2.06*
7.	Child Growth (CG)	4.70	3.34	7.15	5.37	1.99[NS]
8.	Hygiene (HG)	3.65	3.19	6.80	3.10	3.09**
9.	Diarrhoea	5.10	3.05	7.60	4.05	2.19*

| 10. | Cold & Cough (CC) | 5.10 | 3.34 | 7.15 | 4.31 | 1.75^{NS} |
| Total | **Population- Health Literacy (PHL)** | 45.40 | 15.66 | 63.95 | 14.72 | 3.81** |

N S = Not Significant

**/* = Significant at 0.01 and 0.05 respectively

N = 20

Similar analyses have been done for the Experimental Group in the age-range of 30-39 years (Table 4.11). The Table presents the percentage of correct responses of urban housewives (30-39) years of Experimental Group in before-after intervention measures of PHL and its dimensions. In earlier analyses of urban housewives (20-29 years) it has been marked that in all the ten dimensions of PHL, as well as in total PHL the knowledge of urban housewives has grown reasonably. There seems to be a sharp difference in the knowledge before intervention and after intervention. The housewives (30-39 years) have also shown the same tendency as marked above invariably in all the ten dimensions of PHL housewives after intervention have shown a good increase in the PHL knowledge. The difference between the knowledge levels of before intervention and after intervention is as high as 31.60% in the case of Cough and Cold (CC) dimensions of PHL. The lowest difference between the two conditions is seen in respect to Immunization (IZ) - a difference of 16.25% only. Thus in all the dimensions of PHL it has been seen that the intervention has played very positive role in the enhancement of knowledge. In total PHL it has raised up to 23.18% knowledge. Thus the role of intervention has been very positive in enhancing the knowledge of PHL in urban housewives.

The percentage shown in table 4.11 has also been graphically represented in Figure 4.5. The figure clearly expresses the trend which has been detailed in earlier discussions. The bars presenting the after-intervention measures are bigger in their sizes in all the dimensions as well as total PHL. This has clearly shown the positive effect of intervention programme in enhancing the knowledge of urban housewives.

Table 4.11

Percentage of correct Responses of Experimental Group in Before and After Interventions of 30-39 years age-group in PHL and its dimensions

S. No.	Dimensions of PHL	Experimental Group		
		Before Intervention	After Intervention	Gain in %
1.	Adverse Consequences of Population	48.30	65.55	17.25

	Explosion on Quality of Life (PEQ)			
2.	Timing of Birth (TB)	47.0	70.60	23.60
3.	Safe Motherhood (SM)	51.0	68.50	17.50
4.	Breast Feeding (BF)	52.6	74.50	21.90
5.	Immunization (IZ)	49.3	65.55	16.25
6.	Supplementary Food (SF)	53.7	72.6	18.90
7.	Child Growth (CG)	50.20	75.5	25.30
8.	Hygiene (HG)	48.20	70.8	22.60
9.	Diarrhoea (DR)	46.70	66.50	19.80
10.	Cough and Cold (CC)	45.20	76.80	31.60
Total	**Population-Health Literacy (PHL)**	**49.22**	**72.4**	**23.18**

N = 20

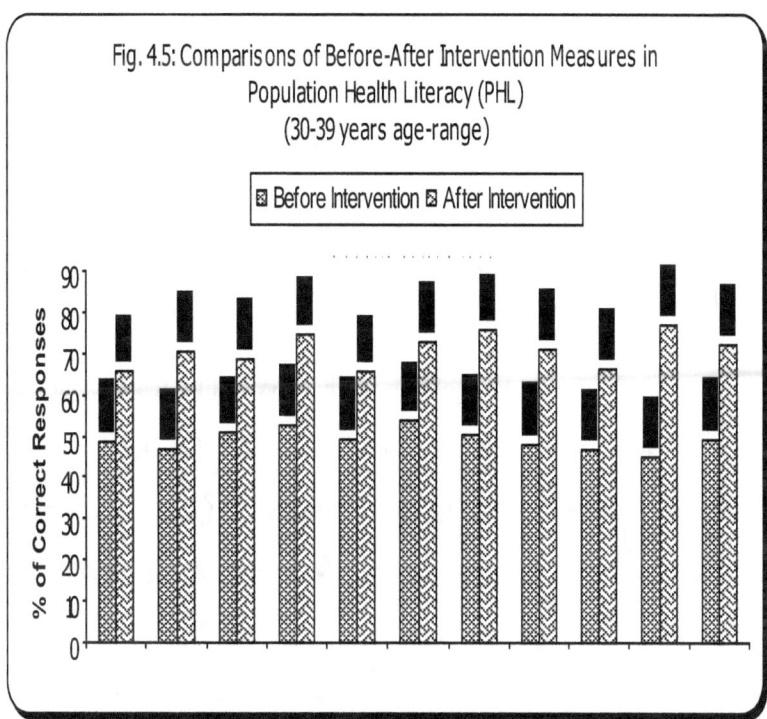

Fig. 4.5: Comparisons of Before-After Intervention Measures in Population Health Literacy (PHL) (30-39 years age-range)

PEQ = Adverse consequence of Population Explosion on Quality of life	TB = Timing of Birth
SM = Safe Motherhood	BF = Breast Feeding
IZ = Immunization	SF = Supplementary Food
CG = Child Growth	HG = Hygiene
DR = Diarrhoea	CC = Cough and Cold
TPHL = Total Population-Health Literacy	

Whether the enhancement of the knowledge due to intervention is statistically significant or not has been further tested by comparing the before-after intervention measures by using t-tests for which the mean scores and SDs in each of the dimensions of PHL have been computed. The comparisons are presented in Table 4.12.

There are total eleven t-values presenting ten comparisons in each of the dimensions and one in PHL. Out of all these t-values a single t-value in relation to Cough and Cold (CC) dimension has been statistically insignificant when other all t-values are statistically significant, though most of them are significant at 0.05 levels only. Only two t-values, one with respect to Child Growth (CG) and another with respect to PHL are significant at 0.01 levels. This has clearly indicated that intervention programme has significantly increased the knowledge of urban housewives in relation to PHL and its dimensions.

As mentioned earlier there are three age-groups of housewives. The analyses of third age-group, namely 40-49 years old housewives have also been made.

Table 4.13 shows the percentage of correct responses of Experimental Group 40-49 years in before-after intervention measures in PHL and its dimensions. A look on the Table indicates here again the same trend of enhancement in the knowledge of urban housewives after intervention programme with respect to each of the dimensions of PHL. Invariably there is increase in each of the areas.

The knowledge of housewives has increased reasonably in relation to PHL after intervention compared to without-intervention conditions. There is as high as of 35.75% enhancement in relation to Timing of Birth (TB). The lowest enhancement has been seen in relation to Cough and Cold (CC) and Safe Motherhood (SM) of 13.90% and 13.80% respectively. Big differences are marked in other eight dimensions of PHL.

Table 4.12

Comparisons of Experimental Group (30-39 years) in Before and After intervention conditions in PHL and its dimensions

S. No.	Dimensions of PHL	Experimental Group				t-values
		Before Intervention		After Intervention		
		M	SD	M	SD	
1.	Adverse consequences of Population Explosion on Quality of Life (PEQ)	6.70	3.62	8.80	2.96	2.00*

2.	Timing of Birth (TB)	5.40	3.56	7.75	3.63	2.06*
3.	Safe Motherhood (SM)	6.35	4.13	8.85	3.10	2.17*
4.	Breast Feeding (BF)	5.95	3.72	8.75	3.15	2.57*
5.	Immunization (IZ)	6.40	4.11	9.20	3.80	2.24*
6.	Supplementary Food (SF)	6.70	3.66	8.90	3.17	2.04*
7.	Child Growth (CG)	5.30	4.03	8.65	3.81	2.70*
8.	Hygiene (HG)	6.65	3.55	9.05	3.70	2.09*
9.	Diarrhoea	5.85	4.14	9.10	4.04	2.50*
10.	Cold & Cough (CC)	6.80	3.74	9.00	4.01	1.80[NS]
Total	**Population-Health Literacy (PHL)**	**62.10**	**18.20**	**87.40**	**14.53**	**4.72****

N S = Not Significant

**/* = Significant at 0.01 and 0.05 respectively

N = 20

Table 4.13

Percentage of correct Responses of Experimental Group in Before and After Interventions of 40-49 years age-group in PHL and its dimensions

S. No.	Dimensions of PHL	Experimental Group		
		Before Intervention	After Intervention	Gain in %
1.	Adverse Consequences of Population Explosion on Quality of Life (PEQ)	28.00	55.10	27.10
2.	Timing of Birth (TB)	24.40	60.15	35.75
3.	Safe Motherhood (SM)	26.80	40.60	13.80
4.	Breast Feeding (BF)	27.80	45.10	17.30
5.	Immunization (IZ)	31.50	50.40	18.90
6.	Supplementary Food (SF)	26.70	45.50	18.80
7.	Child Growth (CG)	31.40	60.70	29.30
8.	Hygiene (HG)	23.90	55.10	31.20
9.	Diarrhoea (DR)	31.10	57.20	26.10
10.	Cough and Cold (CC)	26.90	40.80	13.90

Total	Population-Health Literacy (PHL)	27.25	45.50	18.25

N = 20

Thus the trend seen above confirms the earlier findings reported above in the cases of housewives in the age-range of 20-29 years and 30-39 years. The effect of intervention programme has been clearly marked here too in this age-range of housewives.

The percentages of correct responses discussed above have also been shown through a graph plotted in Figure 4.6. The figure has clearly depicted the findings discussed above. The bars representing the percentage of correct responses of after-intervention measures are quite bigger than those of before-intervention measures. The differences between them in each of the dimensions of Population-Health Literacy (PHL) and total PHL are also high in magnitude. Thus the figure has well revealed the impact of intervention programme through the increased knowledge of housewives in Population-Health Literacy (PHL).

Further tests of significances between the mean differences of before-after intervention measures have also been made by using t-tests. The mean scores, Standard Deviations (SDs) and t-values of housewives in the age-range of 40-49 years in before-after intervention measures of the dimensions of Population-Health Literacy (PHL) have been given in Table 4.14. Out of eleven t-values four are not statistically significant. The t-values in the dimensions of Safe Motherhood (SM), Hygiene (HG), Diarrhoea (DR) and Cough and Cold (CC) are not statistically significant. In rest of the dimensions the t-values are statistically significant. In total Population-Health Literacy (PHL) scale, there exists a significant difference between before after measures. The size of mean scores of after intervention measures suggest that urban housewives have obtained significantly higher knowledge and made correct answers more compared to their performances in pre-intervention conditions. Thus in the third age-range group the similar trend has been found as reported in other two age-group of housewives.

118

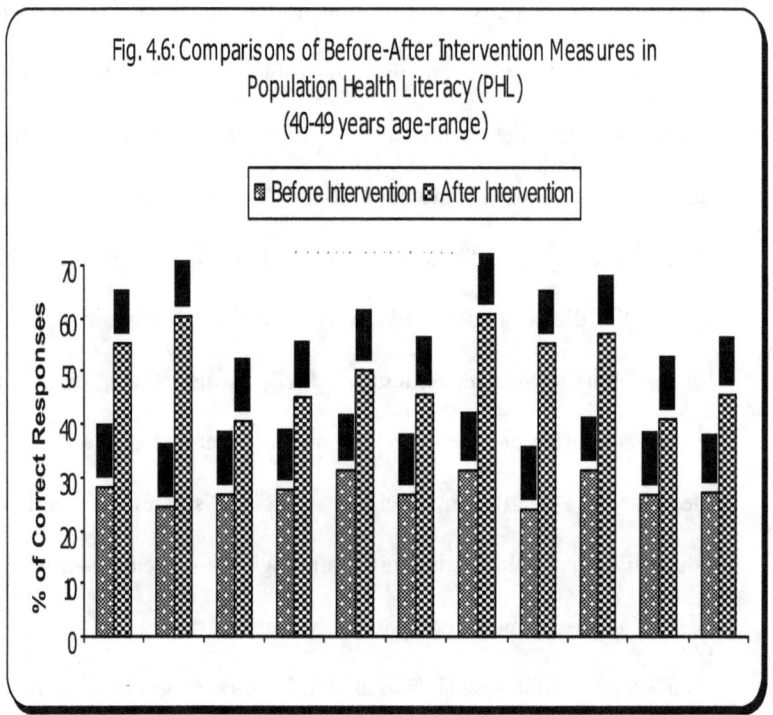

Fig. 4.6: Comparisons of Before-After Intervention Measures in Population Health Literacy (PHL) (40-49 years age-range)

PEQ = Adverse consequence of Population Explosion on Quality of life	TB = Timing of Birth
SM = Safe Motherhood	BF = Breast Feeding
IZ = Immunization	SF = Supplementary Food
CG = Child Growth	HG = Hygiene
DR = Diarrhoea	CC = Cough and Cold
TPHL = Total Population-Health Literacy	

Table 4.14

Comparisons of Experimental Group (40-49 years) in Before and After intervention conditions PHL and its dimensions

S. No.	Dimensions of PHL	Experimental Group				t-values
		Before Intervention		After Intervention		
		M	SD	M	SD	
1.	Adverse consequences of Population Explosion on Quality of Life (PEQ)	5.95	4.37	8.55	3.15	2.15*
2.	Timing of Birth (TB)	6.10	4.05	9.20	3.65	2.54*
3.	Safe Motherhood (SM)	5.30	4.92	8.15	4.13	1.98^{NS}
4.	Breast Feeding (BF)	6.75	4.22	9.35	3.71	2.06*
5.	Immunization (IZ)	4.80	4.15	7.70	3.69	2.34*
6.	Supplementary Food (SF)	5.90	3.63	8.85	4.01	2.44*
7.	Child Growth (CG)	6.30	4.25	9.25	3.47	2.42*
8.	Hygiene (HG)	6.10	3.91	8.55	3.62	1.98^{NS}
9.	Diarrhoea	5.05	4.29	7.45	3.63	1.90^{NS}

120

| 10. | Cold & Cough (CC) | 6.50 | 3.65 | 8.40 | 3.70 | 1.62[NS] |
| Total | **Population- Health Literacy (PHL)** | **58.85** | **17.38** | **85.45** | **15.15** | **5.16**** |

N S = Not Significant

**/* = Significant at 0.01 and 0.05 respectively

N = 20

Taking the total sample of all the three age-groups of housewives the analyses have also been made. However these analyses have been done with respect to total PHL scale. Table 4.15 presents the percentage of correct responses of Experimental Group in before after intervention measures of PHL. The group obtained 32.84% of correct responses before intervention and their knowledge increased up to 52.82% after the introduction of intervention programme in this group. Thus there is a gain of 19.98% knowledge in PHL after intervention programme.

Table 4.15

Percentage of correct Responses of Experimental Group in Before and After Interventions (Total Sample) in PHL and its dimensions

S. No.	Dimensions	Experimental Group		
		Before Intervention	**After Intervention**	**Gain in %**

S. No.	Dimensions				
1.	Population-Health Literacy (PHL)	32.84	52.82	19.98	

N = 60

Further the mean scores and SDs of total sample were also computed for the total sample for before-after measures and the significance between the two mean differences was also calculated. This has been reported in Table 4.16.

It has been marked that there exists significant difference between the two measures. The mean score of after-intervention measure is significantly higher (at 0.01 level) than that of before-intervention measure. The magnitude of t-value (7.20) suggests a high level of significance. It is evident that the effect of intervention was statistically significant.

Table 4.16

Comparisons of Experimental Group in Before and After interventions (Total Sample) in Population-Health Literacy (PHL): t-value

S. No.	Dimensions	Experimental Group				t-value
		Before Intervention		After Intervention		
		M	SD	M	SD	

1.	Population-Health Literacy (PHL)	55.45	19.21	78.93	16.37	7.20**

** Significant of 0.01 levels

N = 60

Various analyses have been reported in Tables: 4.9 to 4.16 and Figures: 4.3 to 4.6 to determine the role of intervention in enhancing the knowledge of urban housewives in Population-Health Literacy. It has been fully confirmed that the intervention programme exposed to Experimental Group has helped them in increasing their knowledge concerning Population-Health related issues. It has worked in relation to all the ten dimensions of Population-Health. The intervention has facilitated in acquiring the PHL among Hindu Housewives.

VERIFICATION OF REAL IMPACT OF INTERVENTION PROGRAMME

In previous analyses and discussion it has been found and confirmed that the intervention programme has influenced the Experimental Group and as a result of which the group has shown an enhanced knowledge in all the dimensions of PHL and total. However a question rises about the guarantee of real impact. Now it is to be seen that the intervention programme has really imparted the knowledge.

One can draw the inference that the enhancement in PHL was due to the influence of other environmental factors, the impact of re-test responses, media and the time that passed. This is a question that may arise in one's mind. For the clarification of this question and the verification of the real impact of intervention programme an approach has been adopted.

It should be remembered here that in the initial stage of the research it has been already mentioned that two independent groups have been selected, one known as Control Group, the other as Experimental Group. The Control Group consisted of urban housewives in three age groups, namely 20-29 yrs, 30-39 yrs and 40-49 yrs, each of the three groups represented by 20 subjects making a total of 60 housewives in Control Group. Similar is the structure of Experimental Group consisting of 60 housewives in three age-ranges as the Control Group.

Further it has also been clearly explained that both the groups are matched in PHL knowledge and any one of these two groups can be used as Experimental Group. Both the groups stand in equal footing so far their initial bench mark data is concerned before any intervention.

Intervention programme has been exposed only to the Experimental Group. The Control Group is deprived of the exposures of the intervention materials. After the intervention materials exposed on the Experimental Group a second response test of Population-Health Literacy (PHL) was taken. The first response (before intervention) and the second response (after-intervention) were compared and the significant role of intervention programme was marked.

Thus before-after Experimental design with a single group has been done in this research. The control condition (before intervention) and the Experimental condition (after intervention) were introduced and data were collected on both the conditions and compared. This was done only with respect to so-called Experimental Group.

Keeping in view the raising question about the real impact of intervention programme the Control Group has also been re-tested in PHL. It should be remembered here that no intervention materials was exposed to the so-called Control Group. However after the intervention programme was implemented on the called Experimental Group both the Control and Experimental Groups were re-tested. Both the groups have been retested after a lapse of three months. During this period the intervention materials were exposed only to Experimental Group and not to the Control Group. There was equal lapse of time for both the groups. Urban housewives selected for both the groups had similar environmental conditions, media exposures and every other thing except that of intervention programme. The re-test data of Control Group is based on without intervention exposures.

The data taken in first test of PHL has been compared with the data taken after three months without giving any intervention to this group.

The mean scores and SDs of first test data and second test data have been computed and t-tests have been used to examine the significance of mean differences of two conditions. The analyses have been done separately for each of the age-groups of urban housewives, which have been reported in three separate tables.

Table 4.17 presents the comparisons of first and second responses of PHL by Control Group (20-29 years age range) without intervention. There are eleven t-values, ten for the dimensions of PHL and one for the total PHL and all of them are insignificant statistically. There exists no significant difference between first and second responses. This has proved that due to lapse of time there is no significant difference. Further it is also revealed that the magnitude of t-values is not high.

Table 4.17

Comparisons of First and Second test responses (without interventions) of Control Group (20-29 years) in PHL and its dimensions

S. No.	Dimensions of PHL	Control Group				t-values
		Benchmark		Second Recall		
		M	SD	M	SD	
1.	Adverse consequences of Population Explosion on Quality of Life (PEQ)	4.50	3.15	4.85	3.42	0.34
2.	Timing of Birth (TB)	4.20	3.25	4.50	3.33	0.29
3.	Safe Motherhood (SM)	3.90	3.65	4.55	3.70	0.56
4.	Breast Feeding (BF)	3.60	3.10	3.85	3.18	0.25
5.	Immunization (IZ)	4.00	2.90	3.80	3.15	0.21
6.	Supplementary Food (SF)	3.80	3.05	3.85	3.13	0.05
7.	Child Growth (CG)	3.20	2.80	3.65	3.15	0.69
8.	Hygiene (HG)	4.10	2.65	4.55	2.91	0.51
9.	Diarrhoea (DR)	4.60	3.06	4.45	3.17	0.15

| 10. | Cold & Cough (CC) | 4.80 | 3.15 | 4.10 | 3.63 | 0.65 |
| Total | **Population-Health Literacy (PHL)** | **40.70** | **14.07** | **42.15** | **14.63** | **0.32** |

All t-values are statistically insignificant

N = 20

Table 4.18

Comparisons of First and Second test Recalls (without interventions) of Control Group (30-39 years) in PHL and its dimensions

S. No.	Dimensions of PHL	Control Group				t-values
		Benchmark		Second Recall		
		M	SD	M	SD	
1.	Adverse consequences of Population Explosion on Quality of Life (PEQ)	6.15	3.65	5.75	3.64	0.35
2.	Timing of Birth (TB)	4.70	3.15	4.95	2.98	0.26
3.	Safe Motherhood (SM)	5.90	4.10	6.20	4.15	0.23
4.	Breast Feeding (BF)	5.30	3.85	5.85	3.31	0.48
5.	Immunization	5.50	3.75	6.05	3.63	0.47

	(IZ)					
6.	Supplementary Food (SF)	6.80	4.32	6.35	3.93	0.35
7.	Child Growth (CG)	6.70	4.14	6.15	3.80	0.44
8.	Hygiene (HG)	610	3.90	5.90	3.72	0.17
9.	Diarrhoea (DR)	5.65	3.70	5.80	3.54	0.13
10.	Cold & Cough (CC)	5.70	4.15	6.10	3.83	0.32
Total	**Population-Health Literacy (PHL)**	**58.50**	**17.04**	**59.10**	**15.52**	**0.12**

All t-values are statistically insignificant

N=20

Table 4.19

Comparisons of First and Second test responses (without interventions) of Control Group (40-49 years) in PHL and its dimensions

S. No.	Dimensions of PHL	Control Group				t-values
		Benchmark		Second Recall		
		M	SD	M	SD	
1.	Adverse consequences of Population Explosion on	5.15	4.10	5.80	4.42	0.48

	Quality of Life (PEQ)					
2.	Timing of Birth (TB)	5.45	3.91	5.65	4.12	0.16
3.	Safe Motherhood (SM)	4.85	3.81	5.55	3.73	0.58
4.	Breast Feeding (BF)	5.25	4.05	6.10	3.94	0.67
5.	Immunization (IZ)	6.10	3.75	6.45	3.83	0.29
6.	Supplementary Food (SF)	5.55	3.19	6.15	3.65	0.55
7.	Child Growth (CG)	4.90	4.17	5.80	4.13	0.68
8.	Hygiene (HG)	5.30	3.65	6.05	3.80	0.64
9.	Diarrhoea (DR)	6.15	4.16	6.35	4.30	0.15
10.	Cold & Cough (CC)	6.10	3.27	5.85	3.68	0.23
Total	**Population-Health Literacy (PHL)**	**54.65**	**19.91**	**59.75**	**18.56**	**0.84**

All t-values are statistically insignificant

N = 20

Table 4.18 gives the comparisons of first and second responses of Control Group (30-39 years age-range). Comparisons have been made in each of the ten dimensions of Population-Health Literacy (PHL) and its total scale. There are eleven t-values and statistically none of them is significant. This clearly reveals that there exists no significant difference between first and second responses after a gap of three months. Lapse of time has no effect. The magnitude of difference between the two means has also been too small.

Table 4.19 presents the comparisons of first and second responses of Control Group (40-49 years age-range). Similar as two previous tables there are eleven t-values in total and all of them are statistically insignificant. This indicates that there is no role of the gap period or environmental factors. Both the responses are alike. Taking together all the three age-groups of Control Group the first and second test responses have also been compared and presented in Table 4.20. Here again it is marked that the first test do not differ significantly from that of second test in PHL. The significance of mean-difference is statistically insignificant.

Table 4.20

Comparison of First and Second test responses (without intervention) of Control Group (Total Sample) in Health Population Literacy (PHL): t-value

S. No.	Dimensions	Control Groups				t-value
		I Recall		II Recall		
		M	SD	M	SD	
1.	Population-Health Literacy (PHL)	51.28	18.02	53.67	17.63	0.74[NS]

NS = Not Significant
N = 60

In the light of these findings let the role of intervention programme be verified and confirmed.

In the case of Control Group there exists no significant difference between first and second tests responses of PHL. There is time gap of three months in between the two tests. During this gap no intervention programme that could enhance the knowledge of PHL has been exposed to the Control Group and thus no change has been seen in second test-response.

On the other hand the Experimental Group which stands in equal footing with the Control Group as far as the initial PHL knowledge is concerned has been tested in PHL two times, first in control condition without any intervention and second in

Experimental condition when the intervention programme was exposed to this group during three months of lapsing gap. While analysing and discussing the role of intervention programme in the enhancement of level of PHL it has been marked that the intervention programme has significantly enhanced the knowledge of urban housewives in Population-Health Literacy (PHL) and significant differences have been marked between the two tests, that is, before – after interventions.

Thus after the analyses and discussions of the data of Control Group it has been well verified that there is exact effect of intervention programme, because both the groups before second tests have spent the same period, one without intervention and another with intervention. The Experimental Group has gained the benefit of intervention. Thus the role of intervention programme in the enhancement of PHL knowledge has been verified as well as confirmed.

These analyses have confirmed that the mere lapse of time or environmental factors do not influence the knowledge of PHL.

TESTING THE SECOND HYPOTHESIS

Here one should be reminded of the main hypothesis which has tried to determine the role of intervention programme

(Population-Health Education Materials) on the enhancement of knowledge of PHL. The main hypothesis of the research reads as:

"The intervention (Population-Health Education) will increase the level of knowledge of Population-Health Literacy among Hindu Housewives of Ranchi"

This implies that there will be significant difference between the group (without intervention programme) and the group (with intervention programme).

Let the hypothesis be examined in the light of the analyses and discussions presented above.

Two groups were used in the research, one as Control and the other as Experimental. Both the groups consisted of three sub-groups based on three age-ranges. Each sub-group was represented by 20 urban housewives. Both the Control Group and the Experimental Group were given PHL questionnaire for measuring their levels of knowledge in Population-Health Literacy (PHL). The analysed data showed that there was no big gap in the percentage of correct responses of Control and Experimental Groups (Tables: 4.1 to 4.3 and Figures: 4.1 and 4.2). Further both the groups did not show significant difference in their mean scores (Tables: 4.5 to 4.8). Both the groups were matched in their levels of knowledge of Population-Health Literacy (PHL).

Then the intervention programme (Population-Health Education Materials) was launched in Experimental Group. After giving intervention exposure to each of the housewives of Experimental Group the retest of PHL was done.

The first scores of Experimental Group taken before intervention (Control condition) were compared with those of taken after intervention (Experimental condition).The comparisons have been made for each of three sub-groups based on age-range. Comparisons have been done in two ways. First the percentages of correct responses of before-intervention and after-intervention knowledge have been compared. Second the significance between the mean-differences of before-after interventions has been tested. All these analyses have already been reported earlier (Tables: 4.9 to 4.16, Figures: 4.3. to 4.6) and thoroughly discussed.

The analyses and discussions made above indicate a vast gap between the percentage of correct responses of before and after interventions. The figures have clearly demonstrated the gaps. Further the t-values obtained from the comparisons of the mean scores of before intervention and after intervention have clearly demonstrated significant differences between the two mean scores.

Thus the trend has indicated a clear positive role of intervention (Population-Health Education Material) in enhancing the knowledge of the urban housewives in Population-Health Literacy and its dimensions.

In the light of these findings the present hypothesis has been fully confirmed and it has also been found that the knowledge of PHL has increased in each of the three sub-groups. Thus the present hypothesis mentioned above has been totally supported.

4.3 AGE DIFFERENCE IN POPULATION-HEALTH LITERACY

One of the aims of the present research was to know whether the urban housewives differing in age-range also differ in their levels of PHL knowledge. A hypothesis based on this aim was also formulated.

It should be remembered here that in the present research urban housewives used as Control and Experimental Groups were classified into three age-range groups, namely, 20-29 years, 30-39 years and 40-49 years age-range sub-groups.

To achieve the above aim the comparisons of different age range housewives have been done on the basis of t-values. If has been tried to test the significance of their mean differences. For this only the data of Experimental Group have been taken. Taking the mean scores and SDs of three sub-groups of Experimental Group before-intervention condition the mean scores have been compared.

Similarly the data taken after the intervention have also been used and the three sub-groups have been compared separately. The analyses have been reported in Tables: 4.21 to 4.24.

Table 4.21 presents the mean scores of three housewives sub-groups of three age-ranges of Experimental Group in before intervention condition. Three types of comparisons have been made here; the sub-group 20-29 years have been compared with the sub-group 30-39 years and also with the sub-group 40-49 years and further in third comparison the sub-group 30-39 years have been compared with the sub-group 40-49 in before-intervention condition. Table 4.22 presents the t-values obtained from the comparisons to check the levels of significance of mean differences. First, there are eleven t-values comparing 20-29 years housewives with 30-39 years housewives in different dimensions of Population-Health Literacy (PHL) and total PHL scale. Out of eleven t-values two are significant at 0.01 levels and another two at 0.05 levels. Remaining seven t-values are not statistically significant. In second comparison, housewives of 20-29 years have been compared with those of 40-49 years. Out of eleven t-values only three are found to be statistically significant at 0.05 levels. Remaining eight t-values are statistically insignificant.

In third comparison, housewives of 30-39 years have been compared with those of 40-49 years. All the eleven t-values in these comparisons are statistically insignificant.

Table 4.21

Mean scores and SDs of subgroups of Experimental Group based on Age-Range in dimensions of PHL and total PHL (Before Intervention)

S. No.	Dimensions of PHL		20-29 years	30-39 years	40-49 years
1.	Adverse consequences of Population Explosion on Quality of Life (PEQ)	M	4.80	6.70	5.95
		SD	2.69	3.62	4.37
2.	Timing of Birth (TB)	M	4.50	5.40	6.10
		SD	2.70	3.56	4.05
3.	Safe Motherhood (SM)	M	3.40	6.35	5.30
		SD	3.15	4.13	4.92
4.	Breast Feeding (BF)	M	3.90	5.95	6.75
		SD	3.30	3.72	4.22
5.	Immunization (IZ)	M	4.20	6.40	4.80
		SD	3.55	4.11	4.15
6.	Supplementary Food (SF)	M	4.05	6.70	5.90
		SD	3.74	3.66	3.63
7.	Child Growth (CG)	M	4.70	5.30	6.30
		SD	3.34	4.03	4.25
8.	Hygiene (HG)	M	3.65	6.65	6.10
		SD	3.19	3.55	3.91
9.	Diarrhoea (DR)	M	5.10	5.85	5.05

138

		SD	3.05	4.14	4.29
10.	Cold & Cough (CC)	M	5.10	6.80	6.50
		SD	3.34	3.74	3.65
Total	**Population-Health Literacy (PHL)**	M	**45.40**	**62.10**	**58.85**
		SD	**15.66**	**18.20**	**17.38**

N= 20 in each age sub-group

Table 4.22

Comparisons of sub-groups based on different age-range of Experimental Group in PHL and its dimensions (Before Intervention)

S. No.	Dimensions of PHL	20-29 years versus 30-39 years	20-29 years versus 40-49 years	30-39 years versus 40-49 years
1.	Adverse consequences of Population Explosion on Quality of Life (PEQ)	1.90[NS]	1.01[NS]	0.59[NS]
2.	Timing of Birth (TB)	0.91[NS]	1.47[NS]	0.58[NS]
3.	Safe Motherhood (SM)	2.54*	1.41[NS]	0.73[NS]
4.	Breast Feeding (BF)	1.92[NS]	2.38*	0.63[NS]
5.	Immunization (IZ)	1.80[NS]	0.49[NS]	1.22[NS]
6.	Supplementary Food (SF)	2.26*	1.58[NS]	0.70[NS]

7.	Child Growth (CG)	0.51^{NS}	1.31^{NS}	0.76^{NS}
8.	Hygiene (HG)	2.83**	2.09*	0.45^{NS}
9.	Diarrhoea (DR)	0.61^{NS}	0.04^{NS}	0.60^{NS}
10.	Cold & Cough (CC)	1.52^{NS}	1.26^{NS}	0.26^{NS}
Total	**Population-Health Literacy (PHL)**	**3.11****	**2.57***	**0.58^{NS}**

*/**: Significant at 0.05/0.01 levels respectively

NS = Not Significant

N = 20 in each sub-group

Thus, in total there are thirty three t-values out of which only seven are statistically significant and remaining twenty six are not significant. This shows that in fact age has played no significant role. It should be remembered here in earlier analyses it has been marked that the housewives belonging to 30-39 years age-range of both the Control and the Experimental Groups have shown some higher percentage of correct responses. However age has not played a significant role. It can be guessed here that housewives belonging to 20-29 years age-range are too matured to know everything about Population-Health Issues, and housewives belonging to 40-49 years are too old to have scientific knowledge of Population-Health Issues. Housewives in the age range of 30-39 years are well matured, have better experience and scientific knowledge more than the first and third sub-groups. The third sub-group seems to be more traditional. This is the reason that age-factor does not have clear role than intervention programmes.

It has been mentioned earlier that in the case of the scores of PHL knowledge obtained after intervention to know whether the impact of intervention is different among the sub-groups, differing in age-range, the mean scores and SDs of three sub-groups have been presented in Table 4.23 and t-values are given in Table 4.24. Three types of comparisons using t-tests have been done as done in the case of before-intervention data. Out of eleven t-values comparing 20-29 years housewives with those of 30-39 years only three t-values are statistically significant, two at 0.05 levels and one, PHL at 0.01 levels.

Similarly, only one t-value in relation to PHL is statistically significant in the comparison of 20-29 years housewives with those of 40-49 years out of eleven t-values. This also suggests that age does not play any vital role in the increase of knowledge in relation to Population-Health Issues.

Table 4.23

Mean scores and SDs of subgroups of Experimental Group based on Age-Range in dimensions of PHL and total PHL (After Intervention)

S. No.	Dimensions of PHL		20-29 years	30-39 years	40-49 years
1.	Adverse consequences of Population Explosion on Quality of Life (PEQ)	M	7.25	8.80	8.55
		SD	3.71	2.96	3.15
2.	Timing of Birth (TB)	M	6.95	7.75	9.20
		SD	4.12	3.63	3.65
3.	Safe Motherhood (SM)	M	6.30	8.85	8.15
		SD	3.65	3.10	4.13
4.	Breast Feeding (BF)	M	6.80	8.75	9.35
		SD	4.20	3.15	3.71
5.	Immunization (IZ)	M	7.60	9.20	7.70
		SD	3.80	3.80	3.69
6.	Supplementary Food (SF)	M	6.75	8.90	8.85
		SD	4.50	3.17	4.01
7.	Child Growth (CG)	M	7.15	8.65	9.25
		SD	5.37	3.81	3.47
8.	Hygiene (HG)	M	6.80	9.05	8.55
		SD	3.10	3.70	3.62
9.	Diarrhoea (DR)	M	7.60	9.10	7.45
		SD	4.05	4.04	3.63
10.	Cold & Cough (CC)	M	7.15	9.00	8.40
		SD	4.31	4.01	3.70
Total	**Population-Health Literacy (PHL)**	M	**63.95**	**87.40**	**85.45**
		SD	**14.72**	**14.53**	**15.15**

N= 20 in each sub-group

Table 4.24

Comparisons of sub-groups based on different age-range of Experimental
Group in PHL and its dimensions (After Intervention)

S. No.	Dimensions of PHL	20-29 years versus 30-39 years	20-29 years versus 40-49 years	30-29 years versus 40-49 years
1.	Adverse consequences of Population Explosion on Quality of Life (PEQ)	1.46^{NS}	1.19^{NS}	0.26^{NS}
2.	Timing of Birth (TB)	0.65^{NS}	1.83^{NS}	1.26^{NS}
3.	Safe Motherhood (SM)	2.38^{*}	1.50^{NS}	0.61^{NS}
4.	Breast Feeding (BF)	1.67^{NS}	2.04^{NS}	0.55^{NS}
5.	Immunization (IZ)	1.33^{NS}	0.08^{NS}	0.01^{NS}
6.	Supplementary Food (SF)	1.75^{NS}	1.56^{NS}	0.04^{NS}
7.	Child Growth (CG)	1.15^{NS}	1.68^{NS}	0.53^{NS}
8.	Hygiene (HG)	2.08^{*}	1.64^{NS}	0.52^{NS}
9.	Diarrhoea (DR)	1.17^{NS}	0.12^{NS}	1.35^{NS}
10.	Cold & Cough (CC)	1.42^{NS}	1.01^{NS}	0.49^{NS}
Total	**Population-Health Literacy (PHL)**	5.06^{**}	4.55^{**}	0.41^{NS}

*/**: Significant at 0.05/0.01 levels respectively

NS = Not Significant

N=20 in each sub-group

In the third comparison of 30-39 years housewives with those of 40-49 years, no t-value is statistically significant out of all the eleven comparisons.

Thus in total there are thirty three comparisons between different age-range sub-groups, out of which only four are statistically significant and remaining twenty nine are insignificant.

The analysed data of after-intervention also indicate that age plays no significant role in the enhancement of PHL knowledge. Sub-groups with different age-range do not differ in relation to PHL knowledge.

TESTING THE THIRD HYPOTHESIS

The third hypothesis of the present research reads:

"There will be no impact of age of Hindu Housewives of Ranchi on the intervention effect i.e. Population-Health Education"

Let the above hypothesis be examined and judged in the light of discussions made above under the title **'Age Difference in Population-Health Literary'.**

Comparisons of the knowledge of different age-range sub-groups of housewives have been made separately in before-intervention condition as well as in after intervention condition reported in Tables: 4.21 to 4.24. The significance of mean-differences has been tested by using t-tests. In the pre-intervention condition only seven t-values have been found to be significant while twenty six t-values were statistically insignificant which indicates that age has no specific role to play in PHL knowledge.

In addition to that, analyses have also been made to examine the role of age-difference in PHL knowledge of urban housewives after intervention programme. All the three sub-groups based on different age-ranges have been compared in PHL knowledge. In three types of comparisons there are thirty three t-values, eleven for each age group. Out of all the thirty three t-values, only four t-values were found to be statistically significant. This clearly indicates that there is no significant role of age in PHL knowledge.

In the light of these discussions it is found that the present hypothesis suggesting no significant role of age in PHL knowledge has been supported to its maximum. Hence it is said that the present hypothesis has been proved and no significant difference has been reported in the housewives of different age-ranges.

4.4 MAIN FINDINGS

In a nutshell, the following main findings have been drawn from the analyses made and followed by discussions:

(i)   Both the Control and Experimental Groups prior to introduction of intervention programme have shown poor knowledge in relation to Population-Health dimensions. Both the groups have hardly given 25% correct responses. Control Group as well as the Experimental Group in the first test have shown almost equal knowledge. Housewives belonging to 30-39 years age have given a bit more correct responses as compared to other two sub-groups in the age of 20-29 years and 40-49 years.

(ii)   The role of intervention programme (Population-Health Education Materials) has been significant. Urban housewives after exposure to intervention materials have given significantly higher percentage of correct responses as compared to before intervention condition. There exist significant mean differences in before-after intervention measures. This trend has been marked in relation to all the dimensions of Population-Health Literacy and its total. The hypotheses made here have been confirmed.

(iii)   The role of age has been found to be insignificant. Urban housewives classified into three age-sub-groups have not significantly differed in PHL knowledge. Age-differences have been marked neither in pre-intervention condition nor in post-intervention condition. A null-hypothesis formulated in this respect has been retained.

Chapter 5

5 SUMMARY AND CONCLUSIONS

5.1 INTRODUCTION

The Population-Health status of India is dismal and depressing as revealed by various Population-Health indicators such as population-growth, life expectancy, fertility rate, birth and death rates, contraceptive prevalence rate, incidence of diseases and disabilities, extent of immunization, etc. A comparison of the statistics on Population-Health indicators of India with neighbouring countries such as China and Sri Lanka reflect the low Population-Health status in India.

India is one of the first countries in the world to introduce a policy intended to curb population growth. In the first Five-Year Plan of 1951 a separate plan for checking the population growth was made. In spite of these attempts the population increased steadily in India and crossed one billion in 2001 census. Now it is expected to double its population and become the most populous country in the world by 2035, leaving China behind as China has been successful in curbing the population growth rate.

As far as the Population – Control of the country is concerned it is not easy to control the growth rate merely by enactment of law by the government until the people living in India, irrespective of caste, creed, religion, culture, language and state do not feel the need of the control and adopt the ways of the controlling the decadal growth.

The Population-Health status of India is lower than many of the countries of the globe. In India five states have been named as "BIMARU" (sick), namely Bihar, Jharkhand, Madhya Pradesh, Rajasthan and Uttar Pradesh.

It is the self-awareness' that will minimize the population-growth and the lack of 'self-awareness' is due to lack of Population-Health Literacy. Sociologists, workers in Population-Health area and researchers have felt wide spread superstitions, ignorance and misconceptions with respect to the Population–Health Issues which work as barriers in the way of Population–Health status improvement in India.

There has been lack of discrimination of Population–Health messages conducive to improve the status of Population-Health.

Development of correct and scientific attitude to mould behaviour in relation to Population–Health Issues is needed. It is essential for effective living and necessary pre-requisite for human and social development. Social Scientists and many researchers have felt the low levels of knowledge of both the tribal and non-tribal women in relation to Population-Health Issues. Even educated women have no correct and scientific knowledge in this area.

Therefore if we want to control the population explosion in our country it is needed to educate the mass in general and particularly women in the area of Population-Health Issues to erase superstitions from their mind and grow their knowledge. There is need to produce Population-Health materials taking even the smallest issue. The different areas of the Population-Health are to be explored. The messages should be prepared to convey to the mass. It is needed to make intervention programmes. The messages should be conveyed verbally, pictorially, in the form of slogans, symbolically, so that may be useful to both literate and illiterate people to enhance their level of knowledge in Population-Health area. This will originate the Population-Health consciousness in them and need for the control of growth rate if they know the consequences of population education.

Some of the studies reported in India have accepted the role of intervention programmes in the enhancement of level of knowledge in the concerned field such as AIDS Education, Cleanliness Education as well as Population-Health Literacy. These studies have confirmed the positive role of intervention programmes

150

(Aziz et al., 1990; Choudhary, 1996; Dhamija et al., 1993; Naqvi, 1995; Rehman, 1994; Singh, 1991).

Inspired by these studies the present research has been conducted to determine the role of education, age and intervention programmes in the area of Population-Health Literacy. The work has been conducted in the urban housewives of Ranchi City, a neglected area. The housewives are deprived of many exposures.

In the first stage of research the initial knowledge level of the housewives have been assessed so that the perfect role of intervention programme can be determined. A questionnaire based on the Population-Health Issues have been used for the assessment of their level of knowledge. The questions are based on the following ten important dimensions of Population-Health:

Adverse Consequence of Population Explosion (PEQ)

Items used in this category of questions try to seek one's knowledge concerning the growth rate of population, birth-rate, ways of controlling births and concept of environment.

Timing of Birth (TB)

Questions used in this category try to seek information about time gap between two births, period in uterus, pregnancy and recovery from birth.

Safe Motherhood (SM)

Items related to safe motherhood ask the questions on labour pain, vomiting during pregnancy and its consequences, problem of anaemia in pregnant women etc.

Breast Feeding (BF)

Questions used in this dimension seek to take the knowledge of the respondent concerning the breast feeding, substitute of breast milk, advantages of breast feeding, duration between two breast-feedings, measures for getting sufficient breast milk.

Immunization (IZ)

This dimension tries to seek information concerning various vaccinations to be given to children, timing, and uses of DPT, BCG and Polio Drops etc. and their functions.

Supplementary Food (SF)

Supplementary Food dimension tries to seek the knowledge about the frequency and quantity of food for children during first three years of life, additional food after breast milk, and harmful effect of food cooked long back for children.

Child Growth (CG)

Items related to this dimension seek information concerning child's weight at different periods in initial stage, energy lost during diarrhoea, knowledge of weight chart, etc.

Hygiene (HG)

Seeking information about measures of cleaning water, frequency of washing the child, other knowledge related to personal hygiene.

Diarrhoea (DR)

Questions related to diarrhoea seek knowledge about the symptoms and consequences of diarrhoea, concept of dehydration and use of ORS, use of other liquid food to small child.

Cough and Cold (CC)

The items under this category are related to measure the knowledge concerning the symptoms of cough and cold, sore-throats, running nose, fear of pneumonia, how to save children from severe attack of cold, etc.

All these dimensions are related to Population-Health which a mother should have the knowledge of for the well-being of health of babies and expecting mothers.

The Population–Health Literacy Questionnaire was applied to the urban housewives of Control and Experimental Groups and their levels of knowledge were measured so that both the groups should be matched in PHL. The Intervention materials were exposed only to Experimental Group. Each group consisted of three sub-groups in three age-ranges, each sub-group represented by twenty educated housewives.

Intervention material includes Population-Health Education slogans, messages and statements. These were conveyed to the housewives belonging to Experimental Group only by lecture and discussion method. The main purpose of the exposures of such materials was to enhance the knowledge of the recipients of messages in relation to Population-Health Issues. The slogans were concerned with the ten dimensions of the Population-Health Literacy. After each member of the Experimental Group was exposed to the Population-Health Education Materials the re-test of Population-Health Literacy Questionnaire was taken. Further the before – intervention measures of PHL were compared with those of after –intervention measures so that the exact role of intervention programme be assessed in the enhancement of knowledge in the area of Population-Health Literacy.

An experimental design has been used in the present research. It has been tried to locate the exact place of intervention and role of age in intervention.

The urban housewives residing in the same town and facing the similar environmental exposures are well matched to be grouped as Control and Experimental one. Further the comparison of bench mark data has well matched them in the levels of PHL before the exposures of Population-Health Education Materials.

In the light of these facts the present research becomes an important one to get a finding more scientifically.

5.2 AIMS

The research has been done with following aims:

1. To collect benchmark data from the educated (matriculation onwards) Hindu   housewives of Ranchi regarding their knowledge about Population-Health   issues

2. To conduct an intervention study using Population-Health Education of Hindu   housewives of Ranchi

3. To examine the impact of age on Population-Health Literacy of Hindu   housewives of Ranchi after intervention

5.3 HYPOTHESES

Based on aims the following hypotheses have been formulated:

1. *The Population-Health Literacy will be low in the Hindu Housewives of Ranchi*

2. *The intervention (Population-Health Education) will increase the level of knowledge of Population-Health Literacy among Hindu Housewives of Ranchi*

3. *There will be no impact of age of Hindu Housewives of Ranchi on the intervention effect i.e. Population-Health Education*

5.4 SAMPLE

The sample comprised of 120 Hindu Housewives randomly selected from Ranchi, the capital city of Jharkhand. The age group of the sample ranged between 20 and 49 years. The sample was selected in two stages. Initially, Personal Data Sheet was applied among 500 Hindu Housewives to fetch their basic information such as name, age, profession, etc. Subsequently, 120 Hindu Housewives were selected on the basis of the classification of three age-groups consisting of 40 Hindu Housewives in each group. The categorisation of three age-groups is as follows:

The age of the first group of Hindu Housewives ranged between 20 and 29 years. The second age category ranged between 30 and 39 years and the third category ranged between 40 and 49 years. Each age-group consisted of 40 Hindu Housewives. All the three age-groups were again classified into categories: Control Group and Experimental Group. Each sub-group consisted of 20 Hindu Housewives. The design of the research has been finalized on the basis of before and after design.

The data was collected in two stages. In the first stage, a benchmark data (Population-Health Literacy Questionnaire) was collected from all the 120 samples, which included both the Control and Experimental Groups. One week after collecting the benchmark data, the intervention (Population-Health Education) was given only to the Experimental Groups, and no information regarding the Population-Health Education was given to the Control Groups.

After three months from collecting the benchmark data from the entire 120 samples, the Population-Health Literacy Questionnaire was again applied to the Hindu Housewives of both Control and Experimental Groups. Here the Control Group was without intervention and the Experimental Group had the intervention of PHE.

5.5 TOOLS

The following tools were used to achieve the objectives of the research:

(i) Personal Data Questionnaire (PDQ)

The PDQ consisted of personal data sheet (enclosed in the Appendix-I). The items chosen were such so as to include the information needed for the research ahead such as identification of the household, number of other female members, their age, marital status etc. The educational level, occupation and income status of the husband were also required in the questionnaire (Appendix – I).

(ii)   Population-Health Literacy Questionnaire (PHLQ)

The PHLQ is the most vital aspect of the study. It is the foundation of the research on which the result of any kind with housewives due to intervention regarding Population-Health Literacy knowledge could be ascertained. The questionnaire covers ten main dimensions or characteristics of the Population-Health Literacy at Ranchi in particular. These dimensions in short are given below about which we have discussed in the prior chapter.

1. Adverse consequences of population explosion on quality of life (PEQ)

2. Timing of birth (TB)

3. Safe motherhood (SM)

4. Breast feeding (BF)

5. Immunization (IZ) / Vaccination

6. Supplementary food (SF)

7. Child growth (CG)

8. Hygiene (HG)

9. Diarrhoea (DR)

10. Cough and Cold (CC)

Each of the above mentioned dimensions covers 10 questions and therefore the questionnaire has 100 questions in all. Each question has three items and out of three only one item was correct. The range of score therefore was 0 to 100. Correct response gets a score of one (Appendix - II).

(iii)   Population-Health Education Materials

The Population-Health Education Materials were used as an intervention factor. The materials covered all the ten dimensions under the present study. These materials were meant for the Experimental Group only (Appendix - III).

5.6   DATA COLLECTION AND ANALYSES

PHL questionnaire were applied on both the groups of selected sample the Control and the Experimental Groups. After first test of both the groups the Population-Health Education Materials were used only on Experimental Group. The lecture and discussion methods were applied. After the introduction of intervention programme in Experimental Group again both the groups were asked to respond in PHL questionnaire.

The scores of Control Group and Experimental Group before the exposure of intervention materials were compared, the scores of before-after intervention of Experimental Group were compared and finally the first scores of Control Group were compared with those of second scores. It should be remembered that no exposure of intervention materials was given to the Control

Group. Proper statistical techniques have been used for the aforesaid comparisons. Comparisons of sub-groups of experimental group based on age-ranges were also made to ascertain the role of age.

5.7   MAIN FINDINGS OF THE RESEARCH

On the basis of analyses and discussions in previous chapter the following main findings have are as follows:

5.7.1   Level of PHL Knowledge

(i)   The level of the knowledge of Population-Health Literacy has been low in urban housewives of both the Control and Experimental Groups. Hindu urban housewives of lower age-group (20-29 years) as well as higher age-group (40-49 years) have shown very low level of knowledge lesser than 25%. The middle age-group (30-39 years) housewives have shown a bit higher level of knowledge compared to other two sub-groups mentioned above. This trend has been marked in all the ten dimensions of PHL, namely, Adverse Consequences of Population Explosion on Quality of Life (QEP), Timing of Birth (TB), Safe Motherhood (SM), Breast Feeding (BF), Immunization (IZ), Hygiene (HG), Diarrhoea (DR), and Cough and Cold (CC) as well as total

PHL (Tables: 4.1 to 4.4, Figure 4.2). General education played no role.

(ii)   As far as the initial knowledge of Control and Experimental Groups is concerned both the groups have shown equal levels. There exists equality of status is their knowledge of PHL, including its ten dimensions (Tables: 4.5 to 4.8, Figure 4.3). A hypothesis formed in this context has been supported.

5.7.2   Effect of Intervention

Positive role of intervention programme (exposure of Population-Health Education Materials) to the Experimental Group has been clearly marked. Experimental Groups after intervention has given significantly higher percentage of correct responses in PHL and its dimensions. Further the significance of mean differences between the mean scores of before and after intervention test have been clearly statistically significant. This trend has been marked in all the three subgroups based on age of the Experimental Group with respect to all the dimensions of PHL and total scale (Tables 4.9 to 4.16, Figures 4.4 to 4.6). On the other hand comparisons of the scores of first and second tests of Control Group without the exposure of intervention material have shown no significant differences. This result has been marked in all the three subgroups of Control Group (Tables 4.17 to 4.20).

A hypothesis formulated in relation to the role of enhancement of knowledge in PHL has been supported and proved.

5.7.3   Age and PHL

Age plays no significant effect on the level of PHL knowledge. Three subgroups based on age-ranges of Experimental Group before interventions were compared and no significant differences were reported. Similarly these three subgroups after the exposure of intervention materials were compared again and no significant differences were reported (Tables 4.21 to 4.24). A null-hypothesis formulated in this concern was retained and supported.

5.8   THE PRESENT RESEARCH: A CRITIQUE

The present research has clearly revealed the role of intervention programme in the improvement of Population-Health Literacy in the Urban Hindu Housewives.

Based on an experimental design the outcome of the research has been very useful. This will particularly help the social workers, social scientists, and others working in the area of Population-Health Literacy.

The role of intervention has been established in a scientific way using experimental procedure and controlling the relevant variables.

The researcher has tried her level best to keep the things in proper way. However the researcher is not unaware of the limitations of the social researches. In spite of all precautions it has been felt that the present research is not totally free from limitations. There are some of the limitations which have been unhesitatingly accepted by the researcher.

5.9   LIMITATIONS OF THE PRESENT STUDY

The following limitations have been marked:

(i)   The present research is based on a sample of urban housewives who have read up to matriculation level or above. A sample from non-educated group would   have given more knowledge about the intervention.

(ii)   The Researcher has used lecture and discussion method for the exposure of intervention materials. It has been felt that an audio-visual method of exposure would have been more useful for the intervention.

(iii) The intervention in the present research has been given for a single time. The researcher has felt that there should be a use of repeated intervention and response tests to examine the role of first, second or third interventions as the case maybe.

(iv) The Researcher has felt that there is a need to take a sample of housewives from the remote village areas. The present research sample is based in urbanites. The sample of rural areas and illiterates would have given more vivid picture of the impact of intervention.

(v) The PHL scale consists of all possible dimensions of Population-Health Issues. It should have been supplemented with the information of conception of a child, sex-determination and ways of controlling births etc. to make it more useful. These are some of the limitations which have been felt by the Researcher.

5.10 SUGGESTIONS FOR FUTURE RESEARCHES IN PHL

The Researcher feels her responsibility to suggest the following points to the other researchers doing researches in the area of PHL:

(i) A sample from non-educated persons should be included so that the role of intervention is examined thoroughly.

(ii) There is a need to use audio-visual device for the exposure of intervention materials to create interests in the respondents.

(iii) The role of repeated interventions should be ascertained. Repeated interventions can be used in the area of illiterates and remote villages.

(iv) The PHL should be supplemented with the items on birth control, conception, sex-determination etc. too. The other areas of health may also be included.

(v) The area of PHL is very vast. Samples from tribal/non-tribal ethnic groups, different religious groups, villagers, and various age-groups may also be considered. There is need to explore more and more in the area so that a thorough principle can be adopted for the use of social workers, social scientists, government and others.

REFERENCES

Aitken, A. (1994). Recognition of a major role: District nurses and health education. *Prof Nurs*. 9(8): 574-6.

Akogun, O.B. (1992). The effect of selected health education schemes on knowledge and attitudes of the Kanuri towards certain parasitic diseases. *Journal of Social Health*. 112(6): 280-5.

Allensworth, D.D. (1994). The research base for innovative practices on school health education at the secondary level. *J Sch Health*. 64(5): 180-7.

Anderson, R.C. and Anderson, K.E. (1994). Positive changes and work-site health education. *Psychol Rep*. 74(2): 607-10.

Arora, A. (1991). Health modernity in rural tribal women in Santhal Pargana. *Ph.D. Thesis*. Post Graduate Deptt. of Psychology, Ranchi University, Ranchi.

Arora, A. and Choudhary, A. (1993). Health Modernity in rural tribal women of Chhotanagpur and Santhal Pargana. *Social Change*, 23(1): 43-55.

Aziz, K.M.; Haque, B.A.; Hassan, K.Z; Patwary, M.Y.; Huttly, S.R.; Rahman, M.M and Feachem, R.G. (1990).

Reduction in diarrhoeal diseases in children in rural Bangladesh by environmental and behavioural modification. *Trans –R-Soc-Trop-Med-HYg.* 84(3): 433-8.

Banerji, D. (1980). Political economy of population control in India: In L. Bondestam, and S. Bergstrom (Eds): *Poverty and Population Control*, London Academic Press.

Banerji, D. (1992). Family Planning in the Nineties: More of the same? *Economic and Political Weekly*, 27(17): 883-887.

Bang, A.T., Bang, R.A., Tale, O., Sontakke, P., Solanki, J., Wargantiwar, R. and Kelzarkar, P. (1990). Reduction in pheumonia mortality and total childhood mortality by means of community based intervention trial in Gadchiroli, India. *The Lancet* 366(8709): 201-6.

Baqui, A. H., Ahmed, S., Black, R. E., Bhandari, M., Darmstadt, G. L., Misra, R. P., Santosham, M. and Singh, J. V. (2008). Effect of community-based behaviour change management on neonatal mortality in Shivgarh, Uttar Pradesh, India: a cluster-randomised controlled trial. *The Lancet, Volume*

372, Issue 9644, 27 September 2008-3 October 2008, Pages 1151-1162.

Basu, A.M. (1984). Ignorance of family planning methods in India: An important constraint on use. *Studies in Family Planning* 15(3): 136-141.

Berger, D., Inkelas, M., Myhre, S. and Mishler, R. (1994). Devloping health education materials for inner-city low literacy parents. *Public Health Rep.* 109(2): 168-72.

Borlaug, N.E. (1990). *Population: A challenge to contemporary development strategies,* New Delhi, Population foundation of India: 5-17.

Bose, A. (1988). *From Population to People,* New Delhi, B.R. Publishing Corporation.

Brindis, C. (1993). Health policy reform and comprehensive school health education: The need for an effective partnership. *J-Sch-Health.* 63(1): 33-7.

Brown, L.F. (1994). Research in dental health education and health promotion: A review of the literature. *Health Educ.* Q. 21(1): 83-102.

Carlson, M.C. (1994). Population policies and reproductivity rights-always in conflict. Reproductive rights concern, setting out the consensus common causes. *Social Change*, 24 (3 & 4): 3-12.

Cayvelas, O.T., Mart I Murales, E., Mavarro Heras (1993). Compliance with long-term drug treatment: The prescription as a means of health education, *Aten Primaria*, 11(4): 182-4.

Census of India (2001). Office of the Registrar General. *Series-1*.

Ceratti, E., Garavaglia, M., Piatti, L., Brambilla, P., Rondamini, G.F., Bolla, P., Ghisalberti, C. and Chiumello, G. (1990). Screening for obesity in a school children population of the 20th zone of Molan and a nutritional education intervention, *Epidemion Prev.*, 12(45): 1-6.

Chen, M.S. Jr., Anderson, J., Moeschberger, M., Guthrie, R., Kuun, P. and Aziharlick, A. (1994). An evaluation of heart health education for South East Asians. *Am. J. Prev Med.*, 10(4): 205-8.

Choudhary, A. (1993). Health modernity in rural tribal women in Chotanagpur. *Ph. D. Thesis*, Post Graduate Deptt. of Psychology, Ranchi Univ., Ranchi.

Choudhary, S. (1996). Population-health-literacy in college female students of Ranchi, *Ph.D. Thesis*, Ranchi Univ., Ranchi.

Choudhary, S. (2001). *Population-Health-Literacy*, New Delhi; Northern Book Centre.

Choudhary, S. and Singh A.K. (1994). Population-Health Literacy intervention in the tribals and non tribals, *Social Change*, 24 (3&4), 55-70.

Conly, S.R. and Camp, S.L. (1992). *India's family Planning challenge: From rhetoric to action. Country study Series* #2, The Population Crisis Committee. Washington D.C.

Darby, B. J. (1993). Summary: School of Education. *Prev-Med.* 22(4): 595-7.

Das, B. (1975). *Embryology of maternity in ayurveda,* New Delhi, Diary Publishers.

Das, Santos, M. G., Moreira, M. M., Malaguias, M. L. and Schall, V. T. (1993). Health education is 1st grade public schools at the periphery of Belo Horizonte, M.G Brazil, II : Knowledge, opinion and prevalence of helminthiasis among students and teachers. *Rev Inst Med Trop Sao Paulo*, 35(6), 573-9.

Davies, S. and Croucher, R. (1993). An investigation into the role of post-natal health clinics in oral health education. *Community Dental Health.* 10(1): 83-8.

Dhamija, S., Sehgal, A., Luthra, U.K. and Sehgal, K. (1993). Factors associated with awareness and knowledge of cervical cancer in a community: Implication for health education programmes in developing countries. *J.R. soc Health*, 113(4): 184-6.

Dieleman, M., de Grool, E. and Mahayo, C. (1994). Health education in Burundi: Peer Education in practice, *Promot Educ.*, 1(4): 11-4.

Donham, K.J., Merchant, J.A., Lassise, D., Popendrof, W.J. and Burmeister, L.F. (1990). Preventing respiratory disease in Swine confinement workers: Intervention through applied epidemiology, education and consultation. *Am-J-Int. Med*, 18(3): 241-61.

Elder, J., Boddy., P. Barriga, Aguilar, A.L. and Espinal, H. (1991). Honduran experience with the control of acute infantile respiratory infections, *Bio-of-Sanit-Panam.* 110(5): 390-401.

Ehrlich, P.R. (1968). *The Population Bomb*, New York, Ballentine Books.

Ehrlich, P.R. and Ehrlich, A.H. (1990). *The Population Explosion*, New York, Simon and Schuster, 15.

Fortmann, S.P., Taylor, C.B. Flora, J.A. and Winkleby, M.A. (1993a). Effect of community health education on plasma cholesterol levels and diet: The Stanford five city project. *Am J Epidemiol* 137(10): 1093-55.

Fortmann, S.P., Taylor, C.B. Flora, J.A. and Jatulis, D.E. (1993b). Changes in adult cigarette smoking prevalence after five years of community health education: The Stanford five city projects. *American Journal of Epidemionology.* 137(1): 82-96.

Ganikos, M.L., Mc Neil, C., Braslow, J.B., Arkin, EB., Klaus, D., Oberly, ED., and White, M.F. (1994). A case study in planning for public health education: The organ and tissue donation experience, *Public Health Report*, 109(5): 626-31.

George, S.M., Latham, M.C., Abel, R., Ethirajan, N. and Frongillo, E.A. Jr. (1993). Evaluation of effectiveness of good growth monitoring in south Indian villages. *Lancet*. 342(8867): 317.

Government of India (1968). *Report of the committee on Basic Health Services*, New Delhi, Ministry of Health and Family Planning.

Government of India (1982). *Statement of National Health Policy*, New Delhi. Ministry of Health and Family Walfare.

Government of India (1990-91). *Year Book*, Ministry of Health and Family Welfare, Family Welfare Programme in India.

Government of India (1992). *The Eighth Five Year Plan*, New Delhi, Planning Commission.

Government of Jharkhand (2011). *http://www.jharkhand.gov.in/New_Depts/healt/healt_intervention2.html.*

Granadillo, D., Salinas, P., Nava, D'Jesus, L., Delgado, J. and Aronddia, J. (1994). Health Education for Mothers in the Catchment area of the EL Liano ambulatory Centre, Merida, Venezuela, *Atem Primaria*, 13(3): 107-10.

Gunay, O., Ozt Urk, A. and Ozt Urk, Y. (1994). The impact of mother's health education on the prevalence of Acute Respiratory Infections in children. *Turk J Pediatr.* 36(1): 1-5.

Gupta, P. K. (2004). The Status of Maternal Health and Child Care in Newly Formed States of Jharkhand, Chhatisgarh and Uttaranchal of India: A District Level Analysis, *Indian J. Prev. Soc. Med. Vol. 35 No. 1 & 2, 2004.*

Healton, C.G., Messeri, P. (1993). The effect of video intervention on improving knowledge and treatment compliance in the sexually transmitted disease clinic setting lesson for HIV health education. *Sex-Transm-Dis.* 20(2): 70-6.

Hillemand, B. (1993). Health education about alcohol: need to abandon a purely quantitative message. *Bull Acad Nat Med.* 117(7): 1115-21; discussion 1121-2.

Hughes, B. R., Altman, D. G., Newton, J. A. (1994). Melanoma and skin cancer: Evaluation of a health education programme for secondary schools. *Health Educ Q.* 21(3): 355-67.

174

International Institute for Population Science (1994). *National family health survey, India 1992-93: Introductory Report.* Bombay.

International Institute for Population Science (1995). *India Summary Report. National Family Health Survey, 1992-93*, Bombay.

Jackson, S.A. (1994). Comprehensive school health education programs: Innovative practices and issues in standard setting. *J Sch. Health*, 64(5): 177-9.

Jayaswal, M. (1989). Health modernity and its correlates in tribals of South Bihar. *D.Litt. Thesis* Post-Graduate Deptt. of Psychology: Ranchi University, Ranchi.

Jeffery, R.W., Forster, J.L., French, S.A., Kelder, S.H., Lando, H.A. and Mc Govern, P.G. (1993). The Healthy worker Project: A work site intervention for weight control and smoking cessation. *Am-J-Public-Health*, 83: 395-401.

Kelder, S.H., Perry, C.L. and Klepp, K.I. (1993). Community-wide youth exercise promotion: Long term outcomes of Minnesota Heart Health Programme and the class of 1989 study, *J. Sch. Health*, 63(5): 218-23.

Kelly, J.A, St, Laurrence, J.S., Stevenson, L.Y., Hauth, A.C., Kalichman, S.C., Diaz, Y.E., Brasfield, T.L., Koob, J.J. and Morgan, M.G. (1992). Community AIDS/HIV risk education: The effect of endorsement by popular people in three cities, *Am-J-Public Health*, 42(11): 1483-9.

Kumar, V., Kumar, R. and Raina, N. (1989). Impact of oral rehydration therapy on maternal beliefs and practices, *Indian-J-Pediatr.* 56(2): 219-25.

Kurtz, M.E., Johnson, S.M., Ross-Lee B. and Narayanan, S. (1990). Knowledge and attitude regarding smoking: A health education experiment with Malay College Students, *Med-J-Malaysia*, 45(4): 319-24.

Laiho M., Honkala, E., Nyyss Onem, U. and Milen, A. (1993). Three methods of oral health education in secondary schools, *Scand J Dent Res*, 101(6): 422-7.

Levin-Zamir, D., Lipsky, D., Goldberg, D. and Melamed, Z. (1993). Health education for Ethiopian immigrants in Israel, *Isr-J-Med Sci*, 29(6-7): 422-8.

Lewis, C. (1993). A cardio-vascular health education program for rural schools, *J Sch Health*, 63(7): 298-301.

176

Lloyd, L.S., Winch, P., Ortega-Canto, J. and Kendall, C.(1994). The design of a community-based health education intervention for the control of Aedes aegypti, *Am J Trop Md Hyg*, 50(4): 401-11.

Lorig, K.R., Mazonson, P.D. and Holman, H.R. (1993). Evidence suggesting that health education for self management in patients with chronic arthritis has sustained health benefits while reducing health care costs, *Arthritis Rhuem,* 36(4); 439-46.

Malgavkar, P.D. (1991). Quality of life and problems of governance, New Delhi: Centre for policy Research *(Mimeo)*.

Mandal, N. (1995). Unemployment and social development in India. In M. Dubey (Ed.) *Indian Society Today*, Har-Anand Poblication: 92-108.

Meincke–Giebrecht, A., Eloto, C. and Hettwer, H. (1993). Health education in developing countries-Indian health promoters in a tuberculosis prevention program in the chaco region of Paraguay, *Gesundheitswesen*, 55(11): 582-6.

Murthy, G.V., Goswami, A., Narayanan, S. and Amar, S. (1990). Effect of educational intervention on defecation habits in an Indian urban slum. *J-Trop-Med-Hyg*, 93(3): 189-93.

Naqvi, N. (1996). Learning and retention of personal hygiene and environmental sanitation education in tribals. *Ph.D. thesis*, Post-Graduate Department of Psychology, Ranchi University, Ranchi.

NIUA (1994). *Urban Environmental Maps*, New Delhi. National Institute of Urban Affairs.

Odonsi, J,K., and Ogan, V.N. (1993). Assessment of the effectiveness of primary healthcare intervention in the control of three intestinal nematode infections in rural communities, *Public Health*, 107(1): 53-60.

Pandandikar, V.A.P., and Umashankar, P.K. (1994). Fertility control and politics in India, *Population and Development Review*, 20: 89-103.

Pandey, M.R., Sharma, P.R., Gubhaju, B.B., Skakya, G.M., Nuepane, R.P. and Gantam, A. (1990). Impact of a pilot acute respiratory infection (ARI) control programme in the rural community of the hill region of Nepal, *Ann-Trop-Paediatr,* 9(4): 212-20.

Parakh, B.S., and Pandey, J.L. (1991), Population education: The Indian perspective. In C. Seshadri and J.L. Pandey (eds.) *Population education: A national source book* Vol. I. New Delhi: National Council of Educational Research and Training: 25-40.

Patel, A., Agho, K., Badhoniya, N., Dibley, M. J., Khadse, S. and Senarath, U. (2010). Infant and young child feeding indicators and determinants of poor feeding practices in India: Secondary data analysis of National Family Health Survey 2005-06. *Food & Nutrition Bulletin, Volume 31, Number 2, June 2010,* pp. 314-333(20).

Paunio, P., Rautava, P., Helenius, H. and Sillanp, A.A.M. (1994). Children's poor tooth brushing behaviour and mother's assessment of dental health education at well-baby clinics. *Acta Odontol Scand*, 52(1): 36-42.

Pinfold, J.V. (1990). Faecal contamination of water and fingertip-rinses as a method of evaluating the effect of low cost-water supply and sanitation activities on faeco-oral disease transmission: A hygiene intervention study in rural North East Thailand, *Epidemiol-Infect*, 105(2): 377-89.

Porru, S., Donato, F., Apostoli, P., Coniglio, L., Duca, P. and Alessio, L. (1993). The utility of health workers among lead workers: the experience of one program, *Am-J-Ind-Med*, 23(3): 473-81.

Quirk, M.E., Godkin, M.A. and Schwenzfeir, E. (1993). Evaluation of two AIDS prevention intervention for inner-city adolescent and young women, *Am-J-Prev-Med*, 9(1) 21-6.

Rajyalaxmi, C. (1991). Health modernity in tribal and non-tribal women in Santhal Pargana, *Social Change*, 21(1), 23-28.

Rasheed, P. (1993). Perception of diarrhoeal diseases among mothers and mother-to-be: Implication for health education in Saudi Arabia, *Soc-Sci-Med.*, 36(3): 373-7.

Rose, V. (1994). Health education for parents with special needs, *Health visit.* 67(3): 95-96.

Rosella, J.D. (1994). Testicular Cancer Health Education: An integrative review, *Health Educ.* Q, 21(3): 355-67.

Safer, L.A and Harding C.G. (1993). Under pressure programme: Using live theatre to investigate adolescents' attitudes and behaviour related to drug and alcohol abuse education and prevention, *Adolescence*, 28(109): 135-48.

Salleras Samarti, L. Alcaide Megias, J., Altel Gomez, M.M., Canela, Solar, Navas Alcala, E., Su ne Puigbo, M.R. and Serra Majem, L. (1993). Evaluation of the efficacy of health education on the compliance with anti-tuberculosis chemoprophylaxis in school children: A randomised clinical trial, *Tuber Lung Dis.*, 74(1): 28-31.

Sanchez, M.J., Puche Tagores, E., Castro-Martin, B., Pastro-Agude , R. And Martinez Ortega, R. (1991). The influence of health education on nutrition, *Aen-Primaria,* 8(11): 938-41.

Schall, V.T., Dias, A.G., Malagurias, M.L. and Das Santos, M.G. (1993). Health education in 1st grade public schools at the periphery of Belo Horizonte, M.G. Brazil. I. Evaluation of the program relative to schistosomiasis, *Rev Inst Med Trop Sao Paulo*, 35(6): 563-72.

Schirm, V. (1993). Cholesterol screening of older persons. Focussing on healthy education, *J. Egypt Public Heath Assoc.*, 68(1-2): 119-24.

Schou, L. and Wight, C. (1994). Does dental health education affect inequalities in dental health? *Community dental health*, 11(2):97-100.

Sharma, R. (1993). Status of urban environment: Delhi, Bombay, Ahmadabad, Vadodara, *Urban India*, 13(2).

Silvestre, A.J. (1994). Brokering: A process for establishing long-term and stable links with gay male communities for research and public health education, *AIDS Edu Prev*, 6(1): 65-73.

Singh, A.K. (1984): Poverty, population and prejudice in India: Implications for human development, *UGC National Lectures*, Ranchi, Post Graduate Department of Psychology, Ranchi University.

Singh, A.K. (1987). Family planning and child care in rural tribals of Chotanagpur. *Social Change*. 18(1), 3-29.

Singh, A.K. and Choudhary, S. (1994). Population of India: Present status and future direction, *Social Change*, 24 (3-4).

Singh, A.K. and Jayaswal, M. (1989). Health modernity in the tribals of South Bihar, *Social Change*, 19(1): 13-29.

Singh, A.K. and Jayaswal, M. (1995). Health modernity in the tribals of Jharkhand, Bihar. In A.K. Singh and M.K. Jabbi (Eds), *The status of tribals in India: Health, education and employment*, New Delhi: Har Anand Publication, 111-177.

Singh, A.K., Jayaswal, M. and Hans, A.(1991). Cleanliness education in tribals of South Bihar. *Social Change*, 21(2): 3-17.

Singh, A.K., Sinha, S.K., Singh, S.N., Jayaswal, M. and Jabbi M.K. (1987a). The myth of the healthy tribal. *Social Change*. 17(1): 3-23.

Singh, A.K., Sinha, S.K., Singh, S.N., Jayaswal, M., Hans, A. and Jabbi M.K. (1988). Population-Health Education in tribals of South Bihar. *Social Change*. 18(2): 3-29.

Singh, K. (1975). *Population, poverty and the future of India*, New Delhi, National Institute of Family Planning.

Srinivasan, K. (1991). The demographic Scenario revealed by the 1991 census figures, *Journal of family welfare*, 37(3): 3-9.

Srinivasan, K. (1995). *Regulating reproduction in India's Population: Efforts, results and recommendations*, New Delhi, Sage.

Stergachis, A. Newmann, W.E., Williams, K.J. and Schnell, M.M. (1990). The effect of a self-care minimal intervention for colds and flu on the use of medical services, *J.-Gen-Intern-Med*, 5(1): 23-8.

Tamagond, B. and Saroja, K. (1991). Effectiveness of an educational programme for the promotion of colostrums feeding. *The Journal of Family Welfare*. 37(2): 40-46.

The Hindu (1994). Water, water, nowhere, *Survey of the Environment*. (Annual) Madras.

Townsend, J.W. (1994). India and ICPD: Reflections on Cairo, *Social Change*, 24(3-4), 13-19.

Trakroo, P.L. (1999). *Background paper* presented at seminar on population dynamics at the wake of the next millennium-choices and challenges. Jointly organises by FICCI and UNFPA, New Delhi.

Tripathy, P., Barnett, S., Borghi, J., Costello, A., Mahapatra, R., Nair, N., Pagel, C. and Prost, A. (2010). Effect of a participatory intervention with women's groups on birth outcomes and maternal depression in Jharkhand and Orissa, India: a cluster-randomised controlled trial. *The Lancet, Volume 375, Issue 9721, 3 April 2010-9 April 2010*, Pages 1182-1192.

Turner, J.C., Korpita, E., Mohn,L.A. and Hill W.B. (1993). Reduction in sexual risk behaviours among college students following a comprehensive health education intervention, *J-Am-Coll-Health*, 41(5), 187-93.

UN (1994). *Population, Environment and Development*, New York, Department of Economic and Social Information and Policy Analysis.

UNDP (1995). *Human Devlopment Report*. 1995 New Delhi, Oxford.

UNICEF (2008). *The state of the world's children*. New Delhi, Oxford.

Varshney, C.K. (1991). Poopulation, environment and resources. In C. Seshadri and J.L. Pandey (Eds.) *Population education: A national source book* Vol-1., New Delhi, National Council of Educational Research and Training 151-183.

Waddington, H., Fewtrell, L., Snilstveit, B. and White, H. (2009). Water, Sanitation and Hygiene Interventions to combat Childhood Diarrhoea in Developing Countries, *International Initiative for Impact Education, Synthetic Review 001, August 2009*, New Delhi, India.

Waller, J.V. and Goldman, L.(1993). Bringing comprehensive health education to the New York City Public Schools: A private public success story, *Bull NY Acad Med*, 70(3): 171-87.

Wassif, O.M., Gendy., M.F. Saleh, M.A. and ej Sawaf, E.M. (1993). Effect of health education programme on knowledge about AIDS and HIV transmission in paramedical personnel working in Benha hospitals, *J Egypt Public Health Assoc.* 68(1-2): 143-59.

Williams, T. and Jones, H. (1993). School health education in the European community, *J-Sch Health*, 63(3): 133-5.

Wilson, J.M., Chandler, G.N. and Muslihatun, Jamiluddin (1991). Hand washing reduces diarrhoea episodes: A study of Lompok, Indonesia, *Trans-R-Soc-Trop-Med-Hyg*, 85(6): 819-21.

186

Witt, K. and Hector, O. (1991). Reduction of the use of hypnotics by health education: Results from a controlled intervention study in a local community, Ugeskr-Laeger, 153(49): 3460-3.

World Bank (1992). *Development and environment*, New Delhi, Oxford.

World Bank (1995). India's family welfare programme: towards a reproductive and child health approach. *Report No. 14644-IN* Population and Human Resource Operations Divisions, South Asia Country Department 11.

****

www.ingramcontent.com/pod-product-compliance
Lightning Source LLC
Chambersburg PA
CBHW070645290526
45790CB00001B/194